A staggering amount of who and what we are carries over from one life to the next. Researchers have found similarities between handwriting, gestures, and manner of walking carrying over from one life to the next.

Most exciting of all, past-life therapists from around the world report that in many cases the unearthing of memories responsible for disorders alleviates them.

This then is the key. Exploring past lives can help you with your present day problems and even enable you to reawaken your own latent skills and talents.

Also by Michael Talbot:

Fiction

THE DELICATE DEPENDENCY
THE BOG

Nonfiction

MYSTICISM AND THE NEW PHYSICS
BEYOND THE QUANTUM

YOUR PAST LIVES

A Reincarnation Handbook

Michael Talbot

FAWCETT CREST • NEW YORK

A Fawcett Crest Book
Published by Ballantine Books

Published in the United States by Ballantine Books, a division of Random House, Inc., New York, and simultaneously in Canada by Random House of Canada Limited, Toronto.

Library of Congress Catalog Card Number: 87-8803

ISBN 0-449-21679-9

This edition published by arrangement with Crown Publishers, Inc.

Manufactured in the United States of America

First Ballantine Books Edition: May 1989

For Carol Dryer, to whom I owe more than words can express

Contents

Acknowledgments ix
Preface xi
Introduction 1

Part One: Exploring Alone

1 *Preparing* 15
2 *The Resonance Method* 27
3 *Dreaming Techniques* 52
4 *Meditation Techniques* 77
5 *Self-Hypnosis Techniques* 96

Part Two: Exploring for Two

6 *Guided Meditations* 107
7 *The Active Imagination Technique* 117

Part Three: Exploring with Professional Guidance

8 *Exploring with a Professional Past-Life Therapist* 125
9 *Exploring with Psychics and Other Metaphysical Sources* 136

Part Four: Closing Words

10 *The Dangers of Past-Life Exploration* 159
Bibliography 165
Credits 171
Index 173

Acknowledgments

It is difficult to acknowledge all of the people who (in one way or another) contributed to the writing of this book, but a few who deserve special mention include: Carol Dryer, Gregory Paxson, Barbara Hand Clow, Carl Llewellyn Weschcke, Dr. Ernest Pecci, Roger Woolger, Jennifer Woolger, Dr. Hazel Denning, Dr. Jeffrey Mishlove, Dr. Fred Alan Wolf, Judith Wolf, Dr. Stanley R. Dean, Jim Gordon, Mary Palermo, Tam Mossman (and, of course, James). I would also like to thank Marcia Richards and Martha Visser for their diligent work in helping me research the book; Michael Pietsch and Liz Sonneborn at Harmony Books for their careful editing; and, of course, Lucy Kroll, my agent and dear friend for being as wonderful as she is.

Preface

In 1981 a Gallup poll revealed that 38 million Americans now believe they've had past lives—about one fourth of our adult population. More and more intelligent, successful people from all walks of life are seriously beginning to consider the possibility that they have lived before. And this growing interest in reincarnation is not limited to the general public. Increasing numbers of psychologists, medical doctors, and therapists are using past-life regression techniques to help people overcome emotional and physical health problems and tap into skills and talents that some believe were first learned in previous incarnations.

As increasing attention is focused on past lives, more people are becoming interested in exploring the issue for themselves, in finding out how to unlock their own past-life memories, as well as in learning what benefits to their relationships, outlooks, and professional lives might come from unearthing these memories.

This book will satisfy these interests. In it you will find step-by-step exercises and techniques for all of the best-known methods for delving into your past lives. These include meditation methods, ways for you to inspire and remember dreams about your past lives, simple self-hypnosis techniques, and guided imagery exercises for two or more people. Included among these is a technique that I have developed myself called the Resonance Method, which is a very simple way of determining immediately and without meditation various possible past-life dramas, geographic locations, and time periods hidden in your unconscious, as well as numerous other pieces of information which may represent your own past-life memories.

Because some of the methods of past-life recall now available can only be done safely by trained professionals, the book also includes advice on how to find a past-life therapist, what sort of training and credentials to look for, and what sort of regression techniques are available for you to choose from.

Whatever your reasons for wanting to explore your previous lives, and whether you believe in reincarnation or not, you will find that the methods given in this book work. With them you will be able to unlock a stream of remarkable stories which now lie hidden in your unconscious mind. Whether you believe these stories are fantasies or actual past-life memories is up to you. It is my hope only that you learn from them and expand your horizons.

Introduction

I believe in reincarnation. I always have.

The reasons for my conviction are simple. For as long as I can remember I have always had memories of former existences. When I was a small child, this resulted in my refusing to call my parents "mother" and "father" until I was five years old, when they gently persuaded me to stop calling them by their first names because I was embarrassing them in front of their friends. My refusal was not due to any absence of affection on my part. I did not have a mature intellectual understanding of what the tracts of strange memories inside my head meant, but I was vividly aware that I possessed a continuity, a history beyond the child's body in which I found myself. So it did not make sense to me to call the two kind people who were taking care of me my parents.

This was not the only precocity that my parents were forced to contend with. They rapidly discovered that they had a child on their hands who insisted upon drinking several cups of strong black tea every day, who preferred sitting cross-legged on the floor to sitting in chairs, and who was fanatically drawn to things Asian. I also recall asking my mother about several ways that I remembered having died before. Fortunately there was no longer any trauma attached to these memories, and my mother was able to dismiss them.

It wasn't until I grew older that I began to understand the import of this strange farrago of memories. By the time I was an adolescent, I realized that I had clear but fragmented recollections of what appeared to be over a dozen different past lives. In a few instances I even remembered names and other obscure but specific details about certain geographic locations. Although it is difficult for me to prove that these spontaneous recollections are actual evidence of past lives, in a few instances the information that came bubbling out of me seemed otherwise of inexplicable origin. As a very small child, after I finished the traditional "Now I lay me down to sleep" prayer taught to me by my parents, I automatically followed it with a request to God "to release the suffering of all conscious beings . . ." It was only later that I discovered that the ending I had given the prayer was of Buddhist origin. Similarly, as a young adult, although I had had only two months of piano lessons as a child, I discovered that with just a few months of practice I was able to play difficult pieces by Chopin and Rachmaninoff.

But to me the most persuasive evidence that my fragmented memories are actual remnants of past-life experience comes not from the place names, the historical facts, or mysterious pieces of information that I remember, but from the fact that when I look back on this succession of memories, I seem to see the germs of many of the elements that make up my current personality. Sketchy though it is, I see an epic story that tells me where many of my faults and positive attributes, my habits, belief systems, and my various strengths and weaknesses began. Just as most people can look back on their childhoods and see events that helped sculpt their current identity, I see a similar progression of self-development over the lifetimes I remember.

I would like to say at this point that I do not have any memories of having been a famous historical personage, nor do I have any tales to relate about having been a pharaoh or even a lesser pope. Indeed, most of the past lives that I remember are relatively undistinguished and have little about them of interest save for the personal significance they hold for me. However, here and there throughout the book I will offer further experiences of my own when I feel that they communicate larger points, or complement the findings and discoveries of other researchers.

My main reason for deciding to write a book on past lives and my personal experiences with reincarnation is the fact that public attitudes about reincarnation are changing. My first inkling of this came in 1982, shortly after I published a novel about the vampire, entitled *The Delicate Dependency*. I was drawn to the subject because I was disappointed that no vampire story I had encountered satisfactorily explored what I considered to be the most intriguing aspect of vampires—their immortality. In spite of the fact that most vampires are portrayed as centuries old, they seemed to me very much like ordinary human beings, except for their penchant for drinking blood. I reasoned that if an individual had truly lived for centuries, his psyche, his perceptions, and even his thinking processes would be radically different. I believed this because I knew how much I had been affected even by my fragmented memories of having lived before.

After the publication of the novel, I was asked to speak to a group of about forty people. During the course of the talk someone asked the inevitable question: "What inspired you to write a novel about vampires?" I fidgeted. Although reincarnation and my own past-life memories had been my inspiration, I had not mentioned any of this in the novel and harbored the fear that I might be viewed as a little odd if I admitted this secret.

Nonetheless, I took a deep breath and answered. For a moment the audience was silent. Faltering, I explained that I felt that I had lived before. I then asked if anyone in the audience felt the same way. To my surprise, after a moment or two virtually every hand went up, as first one person and then another confessed that they, too, possessed fragments of what they believed to be past-life memories. A middle-aged elementary schoolteacher admitted that she seemed to have a vague recollection of sitting on the porch of a plantation and gazing out over the fields. A young real estate agent confessed that he had always had a sense that he had been a soldier during World War II. What impressed me most of all was the growing level of excitement in the room as person after person scrambled for the opportunity to express thoughts and feelings they had previously kept to themselves. I realized that I had unwittingly opened a floodgate.

Another reason for writing a book about reincarnation is that I have spent my life exploring different ways of understanding both past lives and the spiritual workings of the universe. This exploration has included the reading of countless books, conversations with thinkers in scientific and mystical fields, and my own experiences and observations. In addition to assisting me in writing my novels, my research gave birth to two earlier nonfiction books on mystical subjects, *Mysticism and the New Physics* and *Beyond the Quantum*. During the course of my research I have talked with numerous past-life therapists, and with each step I've found more evidence to support what I call the past-life phenomenon.

Some of the most persuasive evidence in favor of reincarnation was offered by the late psychologist Dr. Helen Wambach. Throughout her twenty-nine-year investigation of the past-life phenomenon, Dr. Wambach amassed compelling evidence that she reported in her two books, *Reliving Past Lives* and *Life Before Life*.

One of the methods Dr. Wambach most frequently employed was to hypnotize a group of adults and then ask them standardized questions about their past lives. After hundreds of such group sessions she would compile the data and examine it statistically to see if the responses corresponded more with historical fact, or more with what one would expect if the past-life memories that were surfacing were merely the result of unconscious fantasy.

For example, she would ask all of the adults in her sessions where they had been in A.D. 25. She reasoned that if the responses were only fantasy, most American adults would associate such a time period with Israel or Rome. Similarly, she figured that most Americans would associate the year 1700 with pilgrims and early America, and the early 1860s with stories about the Civil War.

To her surprise, in a statistical sampling of 1,050 regressions most of the responses she got for A.D. 25 involved past lives in Turkey, Pakistan, and around the Indus River.[1] In the 1700s, 63 percent were in Mediterranean Europe and northern Europe,[2] and in the early 1850s, although half of her subjects reported living in various areas in the United States, only three of her subjects mentioned any involvement with the Civil War![3]

Geographic distribution was not the only topic Wambach asked her subjects about. Surveys have shown that given the choice, a majority of Americans would prefer to live life as a male. However, it is a biological fact that at any given point in history roughly half of the human population was male and half female. If the information she was calling forth was the result of fantasy, Wambach reasoned that her survey should show more memories of male past lives than female, but this was not the case. As she discovered, "regardless of the sex they had in their current lifetime, when regressed to the past, my subjects split neatly and evenly into 50.3 percent male and 49.7 percent females lives."[4]

One criticism that has been leveled against reincarnation is that too many individuals claim to remember lives as rulers and other historical personages, and Wambach investigated this facet of the past-life phenomenon as well. However, far from finding a preponderance of lives lived in fantasized splendor, she found that most of her subjects remembered humble and peasantlike previous existences. Indeed, more than 90 percent of the past lives her subjects recalled were lived as primitive food gatherers, nomadic hunters, or farmers, and less than 10 percent recalled aristocratic former lives.[5]

In short, the more Wambach looked, the more evidence she found that the past lives her subjects reported under hypnosis were not the product of fantasy. The circumstances of the incarnations they recalled followed too closely the ebb and flow of history. Not only did they report accurately about the footwear used, the types of foods eaten, and the population densities of the various areas in which they had lived, but Wambach found that even when she regressed groups of people from completely different cultural backgrounds, her statistical data did not vary appreciably.

Evidence such as Dr. Wambach's is persuasive. But as I continued my research of the past-life phenomenon, what impressed me even more than historical correlations was the fact that past-life information has many practical applications. For several decades increasing numbers of psychologists and psychotherapists have found that a host of human ills are treatable through past-life regression.

For example, clinical psychologist and noted past-life therapist Edith Fiore has found that many eating disorders appear to be connected to past-life causes. In one instance Fiore regressed a woman whose craving for salty foods had left her with dangerously high blood pressure and discovered that in a previous life the woman had been a native American boy who had starved to death when his tribe ran out of salt to cure their meat.[6] Another man who had an uncontrollable craving for chocolate whenever the weather got cold discovered that he had been given a cup of hot chocolate in a past life after he had nearly frozen to death.[7] Fiore states: "I now find that almost all patients with chronic weight excess of ten pounds or more have had a lifetime in which they either starved to death or suffered food deprivation for long periods. I've met 'aborigines,' 'American Indians,' 'natives' of deep Africa, and people from many countries who found themselves without food and often water. Starvation in past lives continues to affect the person in the present one, resulting in a compulsion to overeat. One woman patient who had a persistent fluid-retention problem found herself, several lifetimes ago, dying from dehydration and starvation, as well as smallpox."[8]

Eating disorders are not the only problems researchers have connected to past-life causes. Other ills that various past-life therapists have reported include alcoholism, cigarette smoking and other drug addictions, allergies, arthritis, asthma, cancer, depression, diabetes, epilepsy, eye problems, fears, phobias and obsessions, headaches and other body pains, hyperactivity and childhood autism, insomnia, multiple personalities, relationship problems and child abuse, sexual dysfunctions, stress, and nervousness.

Most exciting of all, past-life therapists from around the world report that in many cases the unearthing of the memories responsible for these disorders alleviates them. An incident encountered by Dr. Stanislav Grof, chief of psychiatric research at the Maryland Psychiatric Research Center and assistant professor of psychiatry at Johns Hopkins University School of Medicine, provides a typical example. For years a patient Dr. Grof calls Norbert suffered from severe pains in his shoulder and pectoral muscles. Norbert, a psychologist and minister by profession, sought all manner of professional help, but after repeated medical examinations no source for his problem could be discovered. Finally, in desperation Norbert sought Dr. Grof's help.

Dr. Grof, a longtime researcher in the past-life phenomenon, decided to place Norbert in a state of past-life awareness. After being regressed, Norbert suddenly found himself in the midst of a military battle. From the uniforms the soldiers were wearing, Norbert was even able to identify the melee as one of the battles in Cromwell's England. Suddenly, as Norbert watched the flurry of soldiers around him, he felt a sharp pain and realized that his chest had been pierced by a lance. At last he had found the cause of his mysterious affliction and after regaining consciousness he discovered that his chronic shoulder pains had vanished.[9]

How much of our current physical condition and personality is the result of who and what we have been in previous lives is a difficult question to answer. Even if we put aside the controversial matter of reincarnation, science has long debated the question of how much individuals are the result of what they were born with—their nature—and how much is a result of their environment—the product of their nurturing. The nature versus nurture debate is still going full swing in scientific circles with new evidence constantly being offered by both sides.

Although it is a question that cannot presently be answered, there is still a great deal of evidence to suggest that a staggering amount of who and what we are carries over from one life to the next. Researchers have found similarities between handwriting, gestures, and manner of walking carrying over from one life to the next. Noted California psychic Carol Dryer told me of an experience she had recently in which she told a young woman that in her last life she had been a polio poster girl and that she would be able to locate a picture of herself during that incarnation if she did a little research. The woman looked at Dryer with astonishment and said that not only had she long been troubled by mysterious pains in her legs, but friends frequently chided her and asked her why she "walked as if she were wearing leg braces?" As if this weren't enough, the woman's mother later contacted Dryer and told her that her psychic revelation had also shed light on another incident that had long mystified the family. The mother reported that when her daughter was a small girl and had been told that she had just received her last polio shot, instead of being happy as most children would have been, the girl had screamed and cried and begged for the shots to continue. The mother confessed that this strange behavior had never made any sense to anyone until Dryer's disclosure of the woman's past-life experience with polio.[10]

It is important to note that the alleviation of problems is not the only benefit that can be derived from unearthing past-life memories. Just as I was able to recall a past-life talent for playing the piano, numerous researchers have also reported successfully reawakening past-life skills and talents. For example, Chicago past-life therapist Gregory Paxson discovered unexpectedly that he was able to ski. According to Paxson, the first time he put on skis and stood on the slopes he experienced a sense of exhilaration and familiarity. To the amazement of his friends, Paxson pushed off and negotiated the slopes like an old pro.[11] Paxson attributes his spontaneous proficiency to a past life in which he learned to ski in the European Alps. In a recent conversation he told me that he has reawakened equally astonishing talents in many of his clients. One man recalled a past-life talent for riding horses and became an excellent rider. Similarly, under Paxson's guidance, writer Barbara Clow tapped into a past life which enabled her to become a better public speaker. Clow recounts this intriguing incident in her recent and thought-provoking book *Eye of the Centaur*.[12]

Dr. Hazel Denning, a parapsychologist and practicing past-life therapist for more than twenty-five years, tells of a housewife who came to her following a painful divorce. The woman was devastated. She had three children, no skills, little education, and no job prospects. However, in a state of past-life awareness the woman reported that she had once been a gifted teacher, and Dr. Denning encouraged her to nurture this talent once again. The woman was skeptical, but because Dr. Denning had put her in an altered state in which she had witnessed the previous life for herself, she decided to give it a try. She became a teacher's aide in elementary school and was such a phenomenal success that her confidence quickly returned. "Today," says Dr. Denning proudly, "she's become a recognized authority in special education, and other schools send their teachers to observe her classrooms and her methods. She even teaches special classes on her methods at the university."[13]

This, then, is the key—exploring past lives can help you with your present-day problems and even enable you to re-awaken your own latent skills and talents. Most amazing of all, researchers have found that you do not even need to believe in reincarnation to recall previous lives or to benefit from remembering them. Whatever the explanation, in states of past-life awareness even the most die-hard skeptics discover that they have their own apparent past-life dramas lurking in their psyches, and the benefits of past-life regression remain unaffected regardless of whether they view these dramas as simply "stories" woven by their unconscious minds, or actual past-life memories.

Therefore, although I have written this book from the point of view of a believer, it should be stressed that you do not have to accept the philosophical premise of reincarnation to benefit from the exercises that I have provided. If you prefer, you can look at past-life memories the same way psychologists look at dreams and fantasies, as simply another expression of your mind's inner workings.

As for myself, after all my experiences and my examination of the evidence, I am convinced of the reality of reincarnation. My own memories suggest that we live sequential lives in different times and places and often in connection with the same group of people. Many others share this belief. For example, when asked if she believed in the reality of past lives, Helen Wambach replied, "I don't believe in reincarnation—I know it." When asked why, she stated, "If you are sitting in a tent on the side of the road and 1,000 people walk past telling you they have crossed a bridge in Pennsylvania, you are convinced of the existence of that bridge in Pennsylvania."[14]

I should state here that despite the teachings of some Eastern religions, none of my personal experiences have ever suggested that we reincarnate as anything other than human beings. This does not mean that I can say unequivocally that the reincarnation process does not involve other animal species. It only means that I have not personally experienced any evidence that it does.

I would also like to caution that when I say I believe in the reality of reincarnation, that does not mean I am convinced that reincarnation in any way represents some sort of final truth in our understanding of the universe. If there is one thing that we have learned from the history of science, it is that our theories about the way the universe works are never permanent. Newton gave us one picture about the way the universe works, and it was and is a valid picture. However, Einstein gave us another, and quantum physics—the branch of physics which seeks to understand the behavior of subatomic particles—has given us yet another. None of them are wrong, but each has gone a step farther than the one before.

I believe the same is true of reincarnation as a way of understanding how the universe works. I think that it is a correct picture as far as it goes, but that there are surely even more correct pictures waiting for us in the future. For example, my own experience suggests that we live sequential lives, but science is showing us that there are levels of reality at which our everyday concepts of time break down. Thus, it may turn out that the apparent sequentiality of past lives is merely an illusion, a result of the limits of our current perceptions. Accordingly, some theories about reincarnation take this into account and assert that in actuality all of our lives—past, present, and future—are occurring simultaneously. (More will be said about this in chapter 9.)

My point is that although I believe in reincarnation, I am convinced that in time my current understandings will be subsumed by even larger understandings. It is thus my hope that whether you are a skeptic or a believer you will approach this book with an open mind. Remember that all of the concepts that I present in the coming chapters are only constructs of words and that all constructs of words are tools. Embrace these tools only so long as they are useful to you, and replace them with other tools when their usefulness comes to an end.

I have written this book to help you explore your own past lives. I've found exploring my past-life memories to be both fascinating and rewarding. Using this book, either on your own or with a professional, will open up entire new worlds for you and help you learn more about yourself and those you love.

My advice for using the book is to read it straight through without attempting any of the techniques described. Then, once you're familiar with the range of possibilities available for your exploration, go back and carefully reread the sections you want to start with. When you understand the techniques described, a quick glance at the boldface heads in a chapter will be enough to get you started on your explorations.

Endnotes

1. An interview with Dr. Helen Wambach, *Reincarnation Report* 1, no. 6 (December 1982): 42.

2. Helen Wambach, *Reliving Past Lives* (New York: Harper & Row, 1978), p. 181.

3. Ibid., p. 186.

4. Ibid., p. 124.

5. Ibid., p. 116.

6. Dr. Edith Fiore, *You Have Been Here Before* (New York: Ballantine, 1978), p. 6.

7. Ibid, pp. 94-98.

8. Ibid., p. 6.

9. Dr. Stanislaf Grof, *Beyond the Brain* (New York: State University of New York Press, 1985), p. 357.

10. Conversation with Carol Dryer, February 2, 1985.

11. Margaret Sachs, "Past-Life Skiing," *Omni* 4, no. 8 (May 1982): 112.

12. Conversation with Gregory Paxson, December 3, 1985.

13. Conversation with Hazel Denning, January 22, 1986.

14. Joe Fisher, *The Case for Reincarnation* (New York: Bantam, 1985), pp. 49-50.

Part One:

Exploring Alone

1 ~

Preparing

Although different methods for remembering past lives employ different techniques, a few basic skills and practices apply to all of them. By considering these and making certain preparations beforehand, you will be better equipped to embark on your own journey of past-life exploration, whatever method you choose. This chapter is devoted to some of the things you can do to prepare for your journey.

Keep A Past-Life Journal

One of the most important prerequisites to beginning to explore your past lives is to set up a past-life journal and get in the habit of *using* it. The journal should be loose-leaf so that you can add pages when necessary, and large enough to accommodate a lot of material. You will also want divider sheets or subject tabs so that you can organize the journal into sections.

How you set your journal up will depend in part on your own idiosyncrasies and on which techniques of past-life recall you choose to explore. Some basic organizational suggestions follow.

The Chronological Record

In one section of the journal keep a chronological record of any information you discover that you think may involve a past life. There are several reasons for having this record of the order in which you remember things. First, you may not immediately recognize the meaning of some of the information you unearth, and by keeping a record, you will not forget anything that may later have significance. Second, sometimes the sequence in which your unconscious mind divulges information is important, and the chronological record may help you recognize hidden patterns and repetitions that might otherwise escape your attention. For example, by going back over my own journal notes I discovered that although I was not consciously aware of it, again and again my psychc kcpt rcturning to thc imagc of a falconcr. Sccing this image crop up here and there throughout several years' worth of notes made me start to pay attention to it, and it subsequently became a key symbol in helping me unravel a past life I had had in ancient Persia.

Last, by regularly committing the information you uncover to a journal, you will help communicate to your unconscious mind the seriousness of your intent. Although it is a subject that will be discussed at greater length later in this book, it bears mentioning now that you should begin to view your unconscious mind as almost a separate entity, a secondary and vaster "you," which stands behind the chatter of your everyday thoughts. It knows much more than you do about who you are and what you have been in previous existences, but like a wise old yogi sitting in a cave, it must be persuaded that you are serious in your desire for greater self-understanding before it will help you in earnest with your quest. Since no language speaks more powerfully to the unconscious mind than habit and repetition, by getting into the habit of bringing past-life information up to the surface and writing it down, you will also help strengthen your past-life "remembering muscles."

Different Past Lives

As you begin to remember your past lives, devote a page (or more, if necessary) to each of the different past-life personalities you begin to discover in your unconscious. For example, you may have a heading called the "17th-century priest" or the "Old West barmaid." You may also list personalities that you have not yet pinned down in history, such as the "woman who died in childbirth," the "leather worker," or the "man who died from a sword wound."

It is imperative that you have a loose-leaf journal for this section to allow you to move pages around, because as you gather together a body of potential past-life information, you will most assuredly make a mistake here and there and occasionally confuse or even imagine a few past-life memories. For this same reason you should also always keep an open mind about the various personalities that you list. Do not become so attached to your notion that you were a courtesan in the court of Louis XIV that you cannot replace this sheet in your journal if your unconscious mind supplies you with evidence to the contrary.

Similarly, remember that the only good reason for finding out about your past lives is to grow and benefit from what you learn, and this will not be the result if you allow ego-aggrandizement to become a factor in compiling this section. Be discerning, and remember that your interest in any one of your previous personalities should always be commensurate with what that incarnation has to teach you about your life in the here and now.

Once you have amassed a sufficient amount of information about any given past life, create a subheading in your journal beneath that personality, and then try to answer the following questions:

- What was/were the most important lesson(s) I learned in that life?
- What do I like most about the person I was in that life?
- What do I dislike most about the person I was in that life?

- What negative influences from that life (situations, events, character traits, etc.) are still affecting who and what I am in this life?
- What positive influences from that life (situations, events, character traits, talents, etc.) are still affecting me in this life?
- Are any of the individuals I know in my current life people I knew in that life, and how has our past-life relationship affected our current circumstances?

Goals

After you have unearthed enough past-life information to be able to answer some of these questions, you should devote another section of your journal to the goals and changes that you would like to effect in your current life as a result of what you have learned. For example, if you unearth a past life in which you were a leader, but in your present life you are now a shy person, or unable to manage even simple situations effectively, you should use the information you have uncovered to help you realize that leadership qualities are still latent within you. Thus, in the goal section of your journal you might write, "I would like to reawaken the bravery, assertiveness, and ability to manage complex situations, which I possessed during my life as a naval commander in ancient Rome."

Because of the tremendous potential for past-life information to heal, benefit, and transform your current life, you will want to set aside room for a lot of entries in this section. Category headings and sample entries might look like this:

Past-life strengths, talents, and wisdom that I would like to enhance or reawaken in my current life

I would like to reawaken the ability to play the piano that I possessed during my life in 19th-century London.

I would like to reawaken the psychic abilities that I possessed when I was a seer in ancient Greece.

I would like to call upon the endurance I possessed

during my life as a soldier in World War I to enhance my ability to reduce the stress I experience in my current job.

I would like to call upon the compassion I possessed when I was a Buddhist monk in India to enhance my current ability to love and be generous with others.

Past-life traumas, pains, and negative patterns I would like to heal or overcome in this life

I would like to let go of the great sadness I feel as a result of the persecution I experienced when I was a slave.

I would like to let go of my tendency to overeat as the result of my having starved to death in a previous life.

I would like to heal my inability to love as the result of the past lives I have had in which I was ill-treated.

I would like to heal the fear of flying I have as the result of having died by falling.

I would like to heal the back pains I have as a result of having had my back broken in a previous life.

Things I would like to forgive myself for or atone for in a positive way

I would like to learn how to forgive myself for having been so cruel during my life as a warrior.

I would like to help others more in this life to atone for having been so selfish during my life as a ruthless landowner.

I would like to learn how to be more accepting in this life to atone for the life in which I participated in the persecution of others.

I would like to learn to forgive myself for the guilt I continue to experience as the result of the past life I had in which I had to survive by stealing from others.

Things I would like to heal or forgive in others

I would like to heal my current relationship with my

> husband and forgive him for having brutalized me in a previous life.
>
> I would like to heal my current relationship with my friend and forgive her for the role she played in my death in a previous life.

There are several reasons why writing down your goals will help you in your past-life explorations. First, objectifying them in written form once again helps communicate your desire to your unconscious mind. In fact, sometimes writing down your goal is all the prodding the unconscious mind needs to initiate the processes necessary to fulfill your request. However, this is not always the case and should follow-up work prove necessary—such as further past-life exploration, dream work, or work with a therapist—writing down your goal will at least help set the process in motion.

Second, writing down your goal will also function as a reminder. For instance, you may find that your mind has grown so accustomed to ignoring various pieces of past-life information that it will take a concerted effort on your part to keep some realizations from slipping back into the mists of the unconscious. As you continue to unravel still more information about your past lives in the months and years ahead, the goals section of your journal will help you keep track of continuing themes and threads you might otherwise forget.

Methods of Exploration

There are several reasons for devoting a section of your journal to each of the different methods of past-life exploration you choose. The first is that after you have spent some time experimenting with different methods, you will be able to see at a glance which methods tend to produce the most information for you. By keeping the methods straight, you will also be able to see what type of information each method helps you unearth. For example, although I have found that meditation and the Resonance Method help me remember the most information in terms of sheer volume, the most specific information—people's names, words in foreign languages, and place names—tends to come through when I employ dreaming techniques.

Also, some of the methods for past-life recall explained in this book require a certain amount of note keeping. For instance, the Resonance Method will instantly allow you to compile a vast number of disparate pieces of information, and you will need to write this information down in your journal simply to be able to analyze it and remember it all. Similarly, dreaming techniques rely on your ability to remember your dreams, and dream researchers have found that this process is actually facilitated by journal keeping.

One word of advice: To avoid having to write down the same information in both the chronological section of your journal and in the section devoted to the particular technique you are employing, you may want to develop some system of cross-referencing. For example, in the chronological section of your journal, instead of keeping a verbatim record of every memory you unearth, you might simply enter a one-line summary of the information or experience and then list the journal page where the more complete records can be found.

Set Up a Room for Your Past-Life Explorations

After you have organized your journal, the next most important thing that you should do is prepare a room in which to perform your past-life explorations. Although no special setting is required for dream work or the Resonance Method, you will need a clean, quiet place with a suitable atmosphere in which to practice solitary meditation, meditations for two, or self-hypnotic techniques.

Many schools of meditation recommend setting aside a room for the sole purpose of your journeys into your deep self. If you are fortunate enough to have a spare room, you might consider converting it to a meditation room. However, any quiet room in which you feel comfortable and relaxed will do—though for many people it is inadvisable to use a bedroom because of its associations with drifting off to sleep.

Once you have chosen a place, you should then outfit it in a way that will be conducive to your own personal meditative needs. For example, if you prefer to sit in the lotus position while you meditate you will want to have a cushion. If you prefer to meditate lying down you may want to install a carpet or a beautiful Oriental rug. It is important to remember that there is no single correct way to meditate. The main thing to keep in mind when you prepare a place for exploring past lives is that your goal is to feel relaxed and comfortable. If you need to use pillows to be comfortable, use pillows. If you prefer to lie on a couch, lie on a couch.

You will also want to create a tranquil and meditative atmosphere in the place that you choose. Again, the way that you go about doing this will depend on your personal idiosyncrasies. For example, some people find that constructing a small shrine in their meditation space helps them achieve a feeling of reverence and quietude. Such a shrine might consist of religious icons, pictures of scenes of natural splendor, or simply a vase of flowers. As for the placement of such objects, you might want to arrange them on a shelf or low table set aside for such a purpose. If you have an alcove in which to place a shrine, so much the better, but even just the corner of the room, an area of wall, or a decorative cabinet will suffice.

People have found many settings that help to open the doors into their previous lives. Some are described below.

Lighting

Lighting is especially important. If you are like most individuals you will probably want the lighting to be soft. A candle, a small nightlight, or a lighting source with a dimmer switch are ideal. You will also want the lighting in a place that provides the least amount of distracting glare—for instance, if you find that it is easiest for you to meditate while you are lying flat on your back, you will probably not want your source of lighting to be overhead. You may also find that you meditate best in total darkness—though if you find yourself more prone to drifting off to sleep than into altered states of consciousness, this is a good indication that you should have some light source on.

As you experiment with different lighting situations, you may also try colored bulbs. However, if you do try this tack, you should pay careful attention to the effects different colors of light have upon you and avoid those which cause you even the slightest feelings of tension or unease.

Music

I personally prefer to meditate in silence, but many find that soft music is conducive to a meditative atmosphere. Many New Age bookstores have records and tapes designed especially for meditation. Some of these are instructional, though, and this may not be what you are looking for, so read the label carefully. Also, since your purpose is to open your inner self to past-life information, it is advisable to avoid music which is suggestive of a specific culture, as this may influence your past-life explorations and even create false past-life impressions.

Incense

Perhaps one of the most ancient techniques for creating a meditative atmosphere is the burning of incense. It is no coincidence that places of worship all over the world have long used incense for this purpose; for many, a gentle and pleasant fragrance is as lulling and hypnotic a "backdrop" to meditation as the playing of soft music. If you decide that incense may be a useful tool for you to use, sample several varieties and see which one has the most unobtrusive and tranquilizing effect upon you. The ancient Egyptians believed that sandalwood was especially beneficial for meditative states, but every individual will respond differently to different scents.

* * *

In addition to the above-mentioned items, here are some other objects which you may need during the course of your past-life explorations:

A pendulum This can be any small, heavy object suspended on a thread or string that is long enough to allow it to swing freely.

A mirror The mirror should be large enough so that you can see your face and upper torso in it while you are in your meditating position.

A tape recorder To record past-life sessions with one or more people.

A candle To use as a focus of meditation during self-hypnosis sessions.

A crystal pendant To use as a focus of meditation during self-hypnosis sessions.

Three-by-five-inch index cards To write down messages to your unconscious mind during self-hypnosis exercises.

Mentholated salve Any mentholated salve which causes a tingling sensation, such as Tiger Balm or Essential Balm, to stimulate the third-eye region of your forehead when using the Christos Technique.

Clear Your Body

Many people find it helpful to clear their body before beginning a meditation session. You may want to refrain from caffeine, alcohol, and any other stimulants or depressants for at least twenty-four hours prior to a past-life exploration session. Not only can such substances impair your ability to enter or stay in a meditative state, but they can also inhibit your ability to remember your dreams should you choose one of the dreaming techniques given in this book.

Drugs are not the only substances that can adversely affect your meditations. I have found that I can obtain the best results if I also abstain from eating anything for several hours prior to a past-life meditation. This will keep you from feeling drowsy and falling asleep when you try to enter a meditative state. For the same reason you will probably get better results if you do not try to meditate when you are fatigued or have some large problem weighing heavily on your mind. The morning hours are an especially ideal time for meditating.

What to Expect

Every person's past-life exploration is unique. Still, there are patterns common to the start of most journeys. As a rule, if you are not subject to emotional instability or neurosis, your unconscious mind will start by showing you innocuous and gentle memories from your past lives—memories that will present no grave challenge to your current beliefs about yourself. Depending on the method you choose, these memories will vary in their richness and detail. For example, if you start with either the Resonance Method or self-hypnosis, the memories that surface will tend to be fragmented. You may remember an object, a circumstance, or a brief scene from one of your past lives. Dreaming methods tend to produce more complete scenes, and meditation methods, more detailed memories still, even overviews of entire lives.

Previous experience of communicating with your unconscious mind will also affect how detailed your memories will be. For instance, if you are a seasoned meditator, or have long practiced remembering and exploring your dreams, it will be easier for you to leap into involved past-life scenarios.

The subjects of the past-life memories you will first come into contact with will depend entirely on your own psyche. Although it is difficult to predict the nature and sequence of the past-life information you will unravel, a good way of beginning to understand and anticipate the process is to look at the way your unconscious divulges information in your dreams. Although dreams may seem somewhat random and haphazard on the surface, on closer examination they are almost always connected to issues you have been dealing with in your waking life. Sometimes a simple and innocuous daily worry may trigger a dream. On other occasions deeper and more profound issues are involved.

When you delve into your psyche, you will find that the same is true of past-life memories. As with dreams, the past-life memories your unconscious mind will offer up to you are usually responses to issues in your everyday life, sometimes issues of relatively little importance. Sometimes the past-life memories will encapsulate and address the major themes and concerns of your life. Only you—armed with an understanding of your own life and inner self—will be able to sort the wheat from the chaff.

2 ~

The Resonance Method

> Through analysis of your present strong tendencies you can pretty accurately surmise what kind of life you led before.
>
> PARAMAHANSA YOGANANDA, *Man's Eternal Quest*

One of the easiest ways for you to begin to decipher your past lives is simply to analyze your current psychological makeup. Many past-life researchers believe that past-life origins can be found not only for current emotional and physical problems, moods, habits, talents, and ways of relating with people, but even for food preferences, clothing tastes, nuances of personality, facial expressions, and body language. By determining which of these various pieces of yourself are holdovers from other lives, you can begin to formulate certain pictures of who and what you've been before. This is what the Resonance Method will help you do.

Because the Resonance Method does not require you to enter any altered states of consciousness, it is also one of the safest methods of past-life recall and a good technique for beginners.

How I Discovered the Resonance Method

The main skill that must be mastered in order to use the Resonance Method is to learn how to sense what I call "resonance." Resonance is an inexplicable tugging at your heart strings, a special draw that you feel toward some things and not others when there is no logical reason in this life for you to feel the way you do. I first discovered resonance when I wondered whether I had ever had a past life in Italy, and I discovered that something inside me, not quite a voice, instantly told me that I had. I next wondered about Germany, and the same formless knowing gave me a negative reply. Intrigued, I went through a list of countries in my mind and discovered that although I had not consciously realized it, I had a very distinct and special echo of familiarity for certain countries and not for others. I also noticed two other things: First, there was no conscious intellectual rhyme or reason inherent in the list I had chosen; and second, all the countries which I had had past-life memories about since I was a child were included in the list.

I went through a number of other lists in my mind, and again I found the same thing. In each category I had a select inventory of items for which I felt a strange magnetism, and each of these subgroups always included, but were not limited to, the time periods, styles of dress, and other related items for which I already had conscious past-life associations. Slowly, I realized that I had an entire ocean of such "resonances" drifting around in the background of my thoughts. Furthermore, I discovered that when I started placing these resonances side by side, they came together to form a larger picture that corroborated and added to the past-life memories I already possessed.

Sensing Resonance

The most exciting discovery I made about the Resonance Method is that it works with just about anyone, even people who have no conscious memories of their past lives. For example, quiet your thoughts and allow your gaze to linger on each of the cities named below.

New York Paris
London Berlin
Rome Moscow
Vienna Jerusalem

As you do this, try not to think about any conscious associations you may have for any of the cities on the list, but look into the background of your thoughts and see what your soul tells you about each one. If you are like most people, you will find that some of the cities have a special tug on you, while others are merely names on paper. Of course, you must also take into account conscious feelings that you have toward each city. For instance, on one hand you may feel that Paris has a special draw for you, but on the other you may have visited it many times, or been influenced by famous artists who lived there. Nonetheless, if you pay very careful attention to the whisperings of your psyche, you will find that there is still a background *something* that differentiates between even those cities you have logical reasons for feeling special about. You may have sensed it when you first visited the city, either as a pronounced déjà vu or simply as a subtle sense of familiarity or belonging. This is resonance.

One word of advice: Resonance is not something that you have to think about. In fact, thinking tends to get in the way of sensing resonance. Resonance is a "subtle knowing" that manifests best when you have detached yourself from your conscious thoughts. When you learn to look into that portion of your mind in which resonance resides, you will even find that it seems to be a sense of having always known something.

One of the most important things to remember in using

the Resonance Method—and indeed in using any method of past-life recall—is to not jump to conclusions. Just because you have a flash of a face wearing an eye patch does not mean you were a pirate on the high seas. It may mean that you wore an eye patch in a previous life, or it may mean that you saw someone wearing an eye patch in a shirt advertisement and simply forgot that you liked the picture. As you use the Resonance Method, remember one cardinal rule: *No single piece of information means anything.* Pieces of information only start to mean something when they fit together into larger pictures.

For example, using the Resonance Method, you will find that you will quickly amass a large list of possible past-life memories—time periods, geographic locations, occupations, and so on. You must then try to acquire the discerning eye of a lawyer or detective as you go over the list to see if any of these disparate pieces of information link together to form a larger picture. If no larger picture immediately jumps out at you, be patient and don't force the pieces together. If in your excitement you get carried away and accidentally fabricate a false past-life history for yourself, you may prevent yourself from recognizing an actual past-life memory that contains information that would be important and beneficial to you. However, if you are patient and trust your own inner guides, the correct pieces will eventually come together. Remember also that an interest in a specific time, period, or place doesn't necessarily mean you feel resonance for it. Learn to distinguish between simple fascination with a thing and the deeper stirrings in your psyche that might suggest something more.

How will you know when you have linked the right pieces of information together? Sometimes you will just know. The meaningfulness and validity of what you have found out will be so obvious that you will be swept with a feeling similar to déjà vu, or an even more powerful emotion. On other occasions you may suddenly realize that eight or ten pieces of information fit together neatly like pieces of a jigsaw puzzle, but when you look at the picture they create, you don't feel anything. Do not be concerned. There may be a reason that you do not want to recognize this particular past-life memory, or it may not be a past-life memory at all. Whatever the case, meditate upon the information, and if it still doesn't mean anything to you, put it aside. If it does contain any meaningful information, sooner or later your unconscious mind will show you the way to understand it.

The best advice that I can give on using the Resonance Method is to imagine that you have stumbled across an ancient fresco covered with mud. As you begin to clean it, you may find a patch of color which suggests that the surface you are cleaning is indeed an ancient artwork, but still you cannot be sure. As you continue to clean, you may find that the patch of color is a shirt-sleeve, and there is a drawing of a hand connected to it, but still you do not know what the picture is in its entirety. Perhaps it is only a graffito. You clean some more and see that the figure is a woman playing a harp, and you continue to wash away the sediment and find what appears to be the trouser leg of another figure standing beside her—but still you do not know the full extent of the panorama you have found until you have cleaned away all of the mud.

The same is true when you are exploring your past-life memories. Even if you use the Resonance Method and uncover quite a complex and coherent past-life story—and you will—do not cling too tenaciously or apply a single interpretation to what you have found. All that you can be sure of is that your unconscious mind has told you something about yourself. Perhaps it is a past-life memory. Perhaps it is something more akin to an allegory or a dream. Whatever it is, it is an important expression of your psyche. Learn from it. Incorporate the good parts of what you discover into your current life, and make peace with anything unpleasant. Then move on.

As you set out to explore your past lives, also remember to keep one foot planted firmly in historical reality. You have probably not been Julius Caesar or Theda Bara or one of the twelve apostles. You have probably not always been the same sex that you are in this life. You have probably not even always been individuals that you would today find likable—

although you should not be afraid to look at the embarrassing or disreputable individuals you have been, for therein lie the most opportunities for growth.

Using the Resonance Method

The past-life places and things for which one tends to have the most resonance are the broader features of human existence. The exceptions to this rule are those things that have left a strong impression in the unconscious because of powerful emotional associations or repeated past-life exposure.

Go through the categories described in the following pages, and every time you find an item for which you feel you may have a past-life resonance, mark it down on a page in your journal. That way you will have all of the fragments of possible past-life memories accumulated in one place so you can study them more easily when you set out to determine if they come together to form any larger patterns.

Cities and Countries

For obvious reasons, most people have powerful resonances for cities and countries in which they lived in past lives. Either run through a list in your mind, or glance at an atlas. In pondering this category it is useful to keep in mind that many place names have changed over the course of time, so the fact that you do not sense any resonance for an area's current name does not mean that you have had no past lives in that area. For example, I do not sense any resonance for Germany, but I do for Prussia, a country that once occupied the northern region of what is now Germany but is no longer in existence. Similarly, you may not feel any resonance for Peking, but Peking was never known by that name to the people who lived there. To overcome this obstacle, you can try conjuring up a strong visual image of an area to see if you have any resonance with the image. You might even try looking at travel books for various regions of the world to see if you come across any images for which you feel a resonance.

You may also discover that you have resonance for places that you can intuitively see, but cannot name. For instance, you might have a special feeling for narrow streets paved in cobblestone, or for farmhouses, or mud-brick buildings, or buildings near water, or spacious city squares, or Gothic spires, minarets, or pagodas. You should keep notes of each of these as well.

In the same vein, you will find that occasionally you will have a powerful resonance for locations that you have no hope of identifying without further information. You may sense that you have lived in a jungle or rain forest during some life, or in a desert. You may feel very close to the mountains, or at home when you are near the ocean. Think about different areas of the world—tropical Pacific islands, rocky northern European seacoasts, Arctic tundra, African velds, rolling Midwest meadows, and snow-covered mountains—and see which of these you have resonance for.

Cultures and Time Periods

Another very rich area of investigation is the various time periods of history. Most people can immediately name at least two or three areas of the past that they have resonance for. Many have a fascination with ancient Egypt, others with the Russian Revolution, Elizabethan times, Biblical times, the American Revolution, the Old West, the Renaissance, 19th-century Paris, the Middle Ages, the Civil War, native North American cultures, Victorian London, Imperial Rome, Mozart's Austria, the Mayan civilization, Genghis Khan's China, the Crusades, ancient Middle East cultures, or Arthurian England. Frequently people can look at the type of books they prefer to read or the pictures they have chosen to put on their walls and discover that they have returned again and again to a specific time period. This is often an indication of a past-life association.

You may also find that you have resonances that you cannot place in time. You may realize that you have a powerful sense of having lived in India, but you may not know enough about Indian history to know when. Or you may have a resonance for having walked among white pillars, but you do not know which ancient culture inspired the feeling. Go back through your thoughts and try to remember any cultural images that tugged at you strangely or which seemed to possess some mote of something that was familiar. These may include a feeling for the stained glass of churches, Japanese paper screens, life in a rural European hamlet, crowded Middle Eastern bazaars, baronial halls filled with red velvet curtains, life in an aboriginal or tribal setting, log cabins, smoky taverns filled with laughter and tankards of ale, stucco buildings and dusty, unpaved streets, huge balls with women in billowing dresses, lean-tos of branches covered with animal skins, the intrigue of a Far Eastern court, life in tents, quilting bees and barn raisings, caravans with camels loaded down with silk and spices, stone walls hung with tapestries, the arabesques of Islamic mosques, or gathering water from a communal village well.

Hobbies and Taste in Music and Art

The things you have chosen to collect or gather around you in this life can also indicate resonance. Have you always been drawn to things Japanese? Do you collect arrowheads, World War I mementos, pictures of sailing ships, Mexican pottery, French porcelain, African statuary, Victorian cameos, objects from Colonial America, Persian carpets, 1920s memorabilia, Civil War coins, books about ancient Greece or Russia's imperial past? Have you always been fascinated by suits of armor or more comfortable if you have a stick of incense burning in the house?

As a school project or hobby did you ever feel drawn to constructing some unusual object, or perhaps some aspect of human life that was not from your current existence? For example, after I began to pay more attention to my past-life memories, I looked back over my childhood and saw that I had made a number of objects that were further expressions of the previous incarnations I was remembering, such as a small model of a medieval French monastery and a papier-mâché sculpture of a Cambodian temple attendant replete with elaborate headdress. Dr. Ian Stevenson, a psychiatrist at the University of Virginia Medical School who has spent nearly three decades collecting and analyzing the case histories of children with past-life memories, writes of children who construct models of objects or scenes from their previous existences, such as a small boy in India who persisted in constructing models of a biscuit and confectionery shop he had owned in a former life.[1]

Some of your tastes in music and art may also be the result of past-life associations. You may find that you have always been unusually drawn to Chinese art, or to the painting of a particular time period, such as medieval art, 19th-century French art, or Egyptian sculpture. Don't be afraid to thumb through art books or consider art from widely disparate origins and periods such as African, Flemish, Babylonian, Renaissance, Indian, Art Nouveau, Greek, Islamic, Native American, Prehistoric, or Mayan art.

Examine your preferences and see if you have always had an unusual affinity for the music of a particular era of history. Just as we tend to associate various pieces of music with certain powerful events from our past in this life, specific pieces can also trigger past-life memories. For example, as a teenager, the first time I heard Rachmaninoff's *Vocalise* I felt such a deep pull and sense of familiarity during a certain passage of the piece that I knew it had held some potent meaning for me during a previous life. By listening to the music while I meditated, I was able to evoke fragmentary images and pieces of information that were later corroborated by other past-life exploration techniques.

The potential for music to trigger past-life remembrances need not always be so specific. For instance, you may find that the music of a particular time period holds resonance for you, such as the music of the Baroque era, the music of the 1920s, or church choir music. Remember, as with everything in this section, no single item means anything by itself. But if you find that through your tastes in art and music, and other preferences, you have repeatedly gravitated toward the same culture or time period, you have probably started to reveal an area of your own past-life fresco.

Race and Skin Color

Once you learn to sense resonance, you can quickly determine certain skin colors and racial origins you have had in past lives. You may find that you have a powerful sense of having been a native American, an Asian, or some other race that you are not in this life.

Furniture, Costumes, and Objects of Different Time Periods

Objects that were cherished or frequently used in a former life seem to have a special power to evoke a feeling of resonance. Stevenson frequently writes of children suddenly recognizing watches, embroidered cushions, and other mundane objects that either belonged to or are similar to ones owned by their former personalities. He has found that exposure to such objects greatly increases the number of details the children remember about their previous lives, and concludes that such instances are the "exemplification of the psychological 'law' that recognition is stronger than recall."[2]

The law is by no means new. For many centuries in Tibet, objects owned by important personages, such as the Dalai Lama and other chosen members of the ecclesiastic aristocracy, would be used to encourage past-life recall in a child thought to be the reincarnation of that departed individual. Generally about two years after the death of the lama in question, a search would be launched throughout the countryside. Often psychics would be consulted, or predictions made by the departed lama himself would be called upon to assist in the search. Once a likely child candidate was found, an array of objects would be placed before him. Some of the objects would be prized possessions of the departed lama. Others would not. If the child quickly and accurately identified only those objects belonging to the deceased lama, it was considered a first step toward authentication.

It should be noted that the deceased lama, or *tulku*, often left behind prosperous estates, and sometimes the stewards of the estates responsible for mounting the search were less than enthusiastic about finding their old employer. Thus, the child believed to be heir was put through rigorous tests before the reins of power were once again handed over.

Nonetheless, the evidence was often so overwhelming that many a hapless steward found he had no choice. In her 1929 book *Magic and Mystery in Tibet*, the explorer and eminent authority on Buddhism, Alexandra David-Neel, told of one instance in which a steward stopped at a farmhouse to ask for a drink of water and suddenly found himself assaulted by a little boy who demanded his jade snuffbox back. The steward was thunderstruck, for he did indeed have in his possession a jade snuffbox that had belonged to his recently departed master. Subsequent tests convinced him that the child was the incarnate lama.

David-Neel herself was present when the child returned triumphant to "his estate," and she watched along with the rest of the household as the boy complained about the alterations that had been made on his property and demanded various other favorite objects, some of which had been completely forgotten and hidden away in obscure closets by the departed lama before he died.[3] (The interested reader may want to refer to Chogyam Trungpa's *Born in Tibet* in which Trungpa, himself an incarnate lama, describes the paranormal events surrounding his birth and rediscovery.)[4]

In my own experience I, too, have learned many things about my past lives as the result of suddenly recognizing objects that are similar to ones I owned in previous existences. For example, once, after glancing at a magazine advertisement for vodka containing an ornately framed picture of a czar, I suddenly found myself swept with anger and wondering, "Where's my picture of *the* czar?" Wrapped in the same thought was the realization that I had not seen the picture for quite some time. This annoyed me because I knew that the elaborate frame was worth a good deal of money, and I started to fear that its long absence meant that it had been stolen. I was just about to stomp around my apartment looking for it when I suddenly realized that I had never owned such an object, at least not in this life. I have remembered a number of objects I owned in previous lives in this manner.

To determine whether you have had any similar experiences, only perhaps at a more subliminal level, think back and try to recall if there have been any objects that struck some sort of deep chord within you the first time you saw them. Perhaps it was a saltcellar, a piece of jewelry, a type of clock, a walking stick. Or perhaps you will find that you have always had a special feeling for a certain kind of china or cut glass, for antique candlesticks, rosewood boxes, English riding saddles, wicker baskets, Ming vases, a particular kind of gemstone, or even something as common as coils of rope.

You can also do this with styles of furniture and clothing from different time periods. You may realize that you've always had a resonance for a particular style of rocking chair, for huge four-poster beds, for a certain kind of writing desk you've seen only in movies, or furniture from a specific culture and time. Similarly, if you think about it, you may realize that you know precisely how it feels to lace up high-buttoned shoes, to tie a cravat, wear an uncomfortable Victorian corset, a powdered wig, Elizabethan tights, a hoop skirt, a suit of armor, or a kimono.

You may even flash immediately on some specific article of clothing that you owned in a past life. I've had many friends and acquaintances to whom I've taught the Resonance Method suddenly exclaim, "Oh, yes, I used to own a beautiful red dress," or "I know that I wore something very tight around the neck," or "I had a blue velvet jacket that buttoned up the side." When I broached the subject of using the Resonance Method to determine styles of dress to one friend of mine, an executive at a television network, her eyes grew wide, and she exclaimed, "Oh, my God, yes, my feet used to be bound!" Although she had never realized this fact before, it suddenly became crystal clear to her why she had had so many foot problems in this life. She took off one of her shoes and showed me that, indeed, the bone structure of her foot was still slightly misshapen in the manner of a bound foot.

If you live near an art museum, you may also want to visit its historical costume and furniture exhibits. Once you have acquired the knack of sensing resonance, it is a relatively easy task to pause before a particular costume or piece of furniture and quickly sense whether you have any resonance for it.

Or you can simply examine the style of clothing and furniture you have gravitated toward in this life. Often we repeat ourselves, choosing at least a few of the things in our present environment because they are echoes of previous existences. For example, Wambach reported that she never gave much thought to the fact that she always wore moccasins until she researched a past life of her own in which she had been a Quaker named John Wolman and discovered that moccasins were also Wolman's preferred footwear.[5] A fondness for fine clothing (or an aversion to) may also be a holdover from a past life.

Occupations

Past-life occupations also appear to leave a powerful imprint on people. Frequently, after I have taught people the Resonance Method and raised the subject of occupations, they can immediately recall two or three jobs they have done in former lives. You may find that the idea of life in a convent or life tilling the land has always evoked a certain strange nostalgia in you. Or you may realize that you have a real feel for medicine, the military, for making things with your hands, for fishing, hunting, teaching, writing, carpentry, building clocks, helping others, acting, weaving, public speaking, electronics, or astronomy.

Once you have come up with a list of occupations for which you have resonance, go back over your life and see if this sheds any light on other aspects of your personality. For example, after I discovered that I had resonance for having been a jeweler, I suddenly realized this aptitude had manifested itself frequently throughout my life without my having been aware of it. I realized that I had always possessed a natural tendency to tinker with watches and other small objects. Although I had never cultivated such a reputation, friends and family frequently brought me their broken chain clasps and other jewelry to be fixed. I even remember that as a small boy, I once saw a book on a famous jeweler in a bookstore, and I paused and gazed at it for a second or two as if the information the book contained were calling me—but then I moved on and had completely forgotten the incident until I had my flash of insight about having been a jeweler.

Once you have accumulated a list of occupations and other items for which you have resonance, look back on your life and see if any of your discoveries cause similar streams of disparate facts about your personality to suddenly come together. When this happens, it is further evidence that you have uncovered a possible past-life fact about yourself.

Languages

Affinities for certain languages are another frequently reported holdover from past lives, and resonance for a particular language may manifest in a number of ways. Occasionally, some individuals actually remember certain words from a past-life tongue. If as a child you came up with curious-sounding terms that no one had ever heard of, or if you sometimes hear strange words in your mind, you might try doing a little investigating to see if they are actually meaningful terms from some other language.

However, even if you have not had this experience, by going through a list of languages, you can still readily determine which ones you have resonance for. Perhaps you have already found that there are certain languages that you were able to pick up almost as if they were second nature. Or perhaps you have never learned a particular language, but find that you have always been drawn to it, or able to pronounce what few words you know from it as effortlessly as a native speaker. Conversely, you may find that you have always had an inexplicable and intense dislike for a certain language, and this may indicate that you have had some unpleasant past-life association with that tongue.

Foods

Predilections for certain foods also appear to exert a powerful influence from one life to the next. Stevenson has reported numerous cases of past-life preferences (and aversions) manifesting in the children he has studied. These include not only broad tendencies, such as taste for very spicy food, an inclination toward vegetarianism, and preference for the particular cuisine of a previous incarnation, but also very specific predilections such as a love of pears, biscuits, a particular kind of dessert, or a favorite dish.

As a child I also had quite a number of very powerful food memories from previous incarnations, including a marked tendency toward vegetarianism, a taste for Eastern food centering around rice dishes, and an addiction to strong black tea. I even remembered and yearned for several foods before I had ever encountered them in this life. For years I longed for a hot beverage that I knew I had enjoyed a great deal in a former life, but because I did not remember its name, I was unable to ask for it. It wasn't until I was in my early twenties that I stumbled across a type of Japanese tea made from the twigs of the *kukicha* tree and was thrilled to discover that it was the taste I had searched for for so long.

As an adult, sensing resonance for certain foods is a little more difficult than when one is a child, because adults have a tendency to like so many different foods anyway. But if you pay close attention to your inner voice, you will still be able to detect a few possible past-life affinities. Go over all of your favorite foods, and see if there are any that have always had a special tug for you. Perhaps you are especially drawn to the cuisine of a particular culture, or maybe the taste of a good red wine or a dark stout has always activated a special warmth and sense of appreciation within you.

Religions

Because of the intensity of feeling that usually accompanies spiritual beliefs, most people can readily identify gods and religions they were drawn to in previous lives. You may even find that you have an icon or two from a past-life religion as a knickknack or art object in your house or apartment. Have you always had a special affinity for Buddhism, Christianity, Egyptian gods, witchcraft, Druidism, statues of Shiva, Taoism, or the writings of the Sufis?

In addition to checking various religions for resonance, look at your innate attitudes about religion. Are you more naturally drawn to worshipping in groups or to private worship in your home? Such proclivities may indicate past-life habits of worship. Similarly, look at those religions that inspire an inexplicable aversion in you. Have you always had a mysterious dislike for a certain sect or for religion in general? Such feelings may be the result of past-life persecutions.

Animals

Evidence suggests that a close affinity for a particular type of animal may indicate a past-life association. If you have always had a special attraction for horses, you have probably been around horses in a previous life. If your love of cats borders on an obsession, you may have loved cats in a previous incarnation, or even worshipped them. Try looking through bestiaries or natural history books to find resonances for animals that might give you clues to previous lives.

Climate

One of the more interesting past-life resonances that seems to stay with us is our ability to tolerate a particular climate. Stevenson has found that Asian children who remember past lives as Europeans or Americans are far more likely to complain about the heat in the tropical climates in which they have been reborn than Asian children who remember past lives as Asians.[6] Look for your own resonances in this area. Have you always felt that you belonged in a climate different from the one in which you grew up?

Body Karmas

Research has shown that sometimes injuries suffered during a previous incarnation can still affect the body in this life. Because of this, you can also check for various body karmas or resonances. To do this, think of the various portions of your body, paying particular attention to parts that have given you repeated problems. See if you sense any past-life resonance for those areas.

Unusual sensitivities about certain parts of your body can also indicate body karmas. An aversion to having things pointed at your eyes or head may indicate a latent past-life memory of a head injury. If you are especially sensitive about wearing scarves or items of clothing which fit snugly around your neck, you may have suffered a neck injury in a previous life. Even something as simple as a slight nervousness or overprotectiveness about a certain part of your body may be a clue that will allow you to unlock a past-life memory.

For example, one day I discovered that whenever I got nervous, I had a curious habit of feeling my neck, almost as if I were checking to make sure that it was all right. It suddenly occurred to me that I had performed this strange gesture hundreds and even thousands of times throughout my life but had never been conscious of what I was doing. However, as soon as awareness of the mannerism crept above my threshold of consciousness, in a flash I realized that my throat had been injured in a previous life, and on a subliminal level I was still reliving that trauma.

Phobias and fears can also be the product of past-life traumas. Examine any fears you have, such as a mysterious fear of water, heights, guns, or fire, and try to determine whether these have any past-life resonance for you.

Physical Traits

There is evidence that physical traits, such as skin tone and hair color, may carry over from one life to the next. Stevenson reports that in Burma he discovered a number of children who remember past lives as British or American pilots who died when they were shot down over that country during

World War II, and all of them have fairer hair and complexions than their Burmese countrymen.[7] Stevenson even cites instances in which children still possess many of the facial features of their previous incarnations.[8]

Although scientific evidence of this is sparse, a number of gifted spiritual individuals and great mystics of the past have also asserted that our physical characteristics do not always change much from one life to the next. For example, Paramahansa Yogananda said that just as we can still see traces in adults' faces of the children they once were, we also retain similar traces of facial features from our previous incarnations. However, Yogananda said that we have one feature which changes very little from one life to the next:

> The eyes especially will be like they were before. Eyes hardly change because they are the windows of the soul. Those whose eyes reflect anger or fear or wickedness should try to change, to remove unlovely qualities that hide and hinder the expression of the beauty of the soul. Owing to the change of environment and company, your mind and body change somewhat. But the eyes change little. You are reborn with the same expression in them.[9]

To find resonances in your physical characteristics, try looking into a mirror and meditating on your features, specifically your eyes, for a few moments to see what echoes and ancient familiarities are there.

Personality Traits

Look at all those personality traits that you seem to have been born with. Have you always been peaceful, nervous, drivingly ambitious, haunted by a fear of failure or self-pity? Do you have a tendency toward violent temper? Have you always been religious, or filled with a feeling that you were in this life to help others or to accomplish some important task or purpose?

Examine social issues and see whether you have resonance for any of them. If you find that you have never been directly hurt by racism, but it still makes you fighting angry, perhaps you have been a victim of racism in a previous life. Or if you find that your heart has always gone out to orphans, to the poor, to rape victims, or war refugees, perhaps you have experienced that kind of social injustice before.

Look at how you feel about the opposite sex and at how much of the opposite sex you see in yourself. If you are a man, but have always had a more sensitive or feminine side, you have probably been a woman in a recent past life. If you are a woman, but have always had a more aggressive or masculine side than most women, you are probably being influenced a little by one of your male past lives. Remember, seeing a bit of the opposite sex in yourself is not something to be ashamed of. If reincarnation is a fact, its purpose appears to be to allow each of us to see life from every angle, and to grow into beings far richer and more multifaceted than the narrow boundaries cultural convention sometimes places upon us. To perceive both male and female aspects in your personality may therefore be a sign of growth, an indication that you have broken out of a constriction and have drawn on many sources to become who and what you are in this life.

As you look at yourself and search for further resonances, consider also the major life issues that seem to be facing you in this life. After a little thought, most people find that in spite of the complexity of their existence, their lives still seem to have one or more basic and overriding themes. You may find that your major theme in life is to be loved or have a family. Or it may be to develop yourself as an artist, a healer, a business person, a world leader, to amass great wealth, or to constantly confront situations that force you to deal with jealousy, persecution, or power. If you are very honest with yourself, you may find that your theme has always been to control or manipulate others, to accomplish impressive feats in order to compensate for a bad inner self-image, to suffer, or even to hurt or be hurt by individuals you love. Examine these areas for resonance, for they, too, may be the result of a saga that has been going on for many lifetimes.

Finally, after you have compiled a list of your major personality traits, goals, issues you feel strongly about, and so on, look at the antithesis of each of these things and check that for resonance also. For example, you may find that you have an urge to be a healer in this life to make up for the fact that you were once a warrior and were responsible for the death or injury of many people in a previous incarnation. Or you may find that you are devoted to teaching or the dissemination of information in this life because you have resonance for the fact that you once lived a life in which you were responsible for the censoring of information.

People You Might Have Known Before

If you are like most people, you have probably already sensed resonance for certain individuals without knowing precisely what you were sensing. Just about everyone has had the experience of meeting somcone and immediately feeling a deep and mysterious familiarity. Sometimes the familiarity manifests as an instant feeling of kinship or friendship. Sometimes it manifests as an immediate dislike, but whatever the case, it is often an indication of past-life association.

Once you know what you are looking for, it is relatively easy to sense whether you have resonance for any of your current family members, friends, and acquaintances. When you do this, it is sometimes helpful to try to forget the visual image and relationship you have with the individual in this life. Also put aside their gender, and try not to view them as confined to being either a man or a woman or even any particular sexual orientation. Then close your eyes and see whether you sense any resonance for who and what you feel the person is on the inside, for their essence. Not only should you find the answer to your question waiting in the background resonance of your thoughts, but you may suddenly see an image of what the person looked like when you knew him or her before.

Getting Through to Your Unconscious Mind

Once they have been told how, most people learn to sense resonance so readily they are surprised they never thought about it before. However, if you are one of the few who has difficulty, you may be having a problem detaching from your conscious thoughts. Since learning to detach from the chatter of your conscious thoughts is the key to virtually all methods of past-life recall, you may want to skip ahead to Chapter 4 and practice a few relaxation techniques before returning to the Resonance Method.

If you still cannot sense resonance and feel that detaching from your conscious thoughts is not your problem, you may find one of the following methods of communicating with your unconscious mind a better alternative.

Using a Pendulum

One of the easiest and most time-tested ways of communicating with your inner self without entering any altered state of consciousness is to use a pendulum. Many psychologists teach the technique to their patients and find that the information thus obtained is remarkably accurate. In his book *Self-Hypnotism*, clinical psychologist Leslie M. LeCron tells of one study in which 402 pregnant women were asked to use a pendulum to determine the sex of their unborn child. According to LeCron, 360 obtained information with a pendulum that ultimately proved correct, including 3 mothers for whom the pendulum accurately predicted twins. LeCron notes that the only times the pendulum proved inaccurate appeared to be when the mothers did not properly detach from their conscious thoughts and allowed "wishful thinking" to affect their results.[10]

Pendulums have also been used to tap into the unconscious psychic abilities of individuals. T.C. Lethbridge, the late archaeologist and keeper of Anglo-Saxon antiquities at the University Museum of Cambridge, England, claimed to obtain accurate information about archaeological relics by consulting a pendulum. Lethbridge asserted that with a pendulum he could detect a latent residue of anger in a sling stone used in a battle two thousand years ago.[11]

To make a pendulum, tie a small, weighted object, such as a wedding ring, a needle, or a pointed quartz pendant, onto a thread eight to ten inches long. Allow the thread to dangle loosely from your thumb and finger with the elbow planted firmly on a level surface, wrist relaxed. Once you have done this, you are now ready to establish the pendulum's possible answers.

First, ask the pendulum a question which you know has a "yes" answer. For example, you can ask it whether it's Monday. Now wait for the pendulum to respond. As with sensing resonance, it is important not to try to consciously influence the pendulum. Simply relax and allow the pendulum to dangle freely, and soon you will notice that it will begin to move. The pendulum has three basic patterns that it can move in. It can move in a clockwise circle. It can move in a counterclockwise circle. Or it can swing in a diagonal. Usually the unconscious mind will choose one circular direction for "yes" and the other for "no." The unconscious mind can then use the diagonal to indicate that the question which was asked cannot be answered with a simple "yes" or "no." This means that the question should be rephrased. If the unconscious mind still replies with a diagonal, it indicates that either it does not know the answer, or it does not want to answer. You can determine which of these two options is correct by further questioning.

Remember, if your unconscious mind tells you it does not want to answer a question, don't push it. If you like, you may come up with "yes" or "no" questions to determine why the pendulum has warned you away from a certain subject, but never blunder ahead and try to explore regions that your unconscious mind has advised you to leave alone. It makes such warnings for your own good, and it would be foolhardy to ignore its cautions.

To make sure that you have understood the way your own unconscious prefers to respond, ask it a list of questions to which you already know the answers. In formulating these questions, remember that your unconscious mind interprets everything much more literally than your conscious mind. It is not unlike the genie in stories about magic wishes, so your questions should be clear and very carefully worded. Once you have established which movements mean "yes," "no," and "ask again in a different way," you are ready to proceed.

To use the pendulum in the Resonance Method, simply go over each item in the various categories in this chapter, and ask the pendulum to tell you which ones you have past-life resonances with. Individuals who find that they can sense resonance on their own may also wish to use a pendulum to ask their unconscious minds further questions about what they discover. You may want to ask the pendulum if you are ready to explore a particular past-life memory. You can ask it if you are ready to embark on a new method of past-life exploration and get its advice on which one would be best for you to try next. You may ask it if a strange dream you had was of a past life, or if you knew your current spouse in a previous life, or indeed any question about your former incarnations. Remember that the less you try to consciously influence the pendulum and muddy its responses with wishful thinking, the more accurate its replies will be.

Using Finger Movements

Some individuals find that they do not even need to use a pendulum to communicate with their unconscious, but can have their unconscious signal them directly via finger movements. To try the finger movement method, sit in a comfortable chair and place your hands palms down on the chair's arms. Put yourself into a state of relaxation and then proceed as with the pendulum method above. But instead of establishing "yes," "no," and "ask again in a different way," with the aid of a pendulum, ask your unconscious mind to chose one of your ten fingers to represent each response. Some people find that with a little practice they can get their unconscious mind to cause a particular finger to move or twitch for each of the above answers. If you find that you can do this, you can then continue as if you were using a pendulum, but substituting finger movements for pendulum movements.

Once you have familiarized yourself with the Resonance Method you will find that it has many advantages over other types of past-life exploration. Because it requires no elaborate preparation, you can employ it at a moments's notice at virtually any time of the night or day. You can check for resonance when you meet new people, when you go to museums, when you visit new places, attend concerts, look through books and magazines, browse through antique shops, and even when you daydream. This makes the Resonance Method an excellent technique for beginners.

However, because the Resonance Method is so easy and allows you to process so much information, it can also be a valuable adjunct to more advanced past-life techniques as well. It can help you quickly determine time periods and cultures on which you should concentrate further efforts, and it can even help you amass more details about those memories once you have unearthed them.

Endnotes

1. Dr. Ian Stevenson, *Twenty Cases Suggestive of Reincarnation* (Charlottesville, Virginia: University Press of Virginia, 1974), p. 47.

2. Ibid., p. 108.

3. Alexandra David-Neel, *Magic and Mystery in Tibet* (Baltimore, Maryland: Penguin, 1971), pp. 126–27.

4. Chogyam Trungpa, *Born in Tibet* (Boston: Shambhala, 1985).

5. Interview with Dr. Helen Wambach, *Reincarnation Report* 1, no. 6 (December 1982): 44.

6. Stevenson, *Reincarnation*, p. 180.

7. Ibid.

8. Ibid., p.196.

9. Paramahansa Yogananda, *Man's Eternal Quest* (Los Angeles: Self-Realization Fellowship, 1982), p. 227.

10. Leslie M. LeCron, *Self-Hypnotism* (New York: Signet, 1964), p. 37.

11 T. C. Lethbridge, *The Power of the Pendulum* (London: Routledge & Kegan Paul, 1984), p. xiii.

3 ~

Dreaming Techniques

> The question of karma is obscure to me, as is also the problem of personal rebirth or the transmigration of souls. "With a free and open mind" I listen attentively to the Indian doctrine of rebirth, and look around in the world of my own experience to see whether somewhere and somehow there is some authentic sign pointing toward reincarnation. . . . Until a few years ago I could not discover anything convincing in this respect. . . . Recently, however, I observed in myself a series of dreams which would seem to describe the process of reincarnation . . . Since this observation is subjective and unique, I prefer only to mention its existence and not to go into it any further. I must confess, however, that after this experience I view the problem of reincarnation with somewhat different eyes . . .
>
> C. G. JUNG, *Memories, Dreams, Reflections*

After learning how to sense resonance, perhaps the next easiest way for you to make contact with your past-life memories is through your dreams. Although it has long been known that dreams are storehouses of information about our past in this life, there is evidence that they frequently contain a good deal of past-life information as well. For example, in 1981 psychic researcher D. Scott Rogo of John F. Kennedy University in Orinda, California, placed a notice in several psychic-oriented magazines asking interested readers to send him accounts of reincarnation memories they had experienced that had emerged in any way *other* than through hypnosis. In his 1985 book *The Search for Yesterday*, Rogo reported that spontaneous past-life memories which surfaced in dreams constituted the largest group of credible accounts.[1]

New York Institute of Technology parapsychologist, Dr. Hans Holzer, another longtime investigator of the reincarnation phenomenon, has also found that dreams are a frequent wellspring of spontaneous past-life memories. Holzer believes that this is because the mind is less resistant to such information during the dream state than when it is awake and notes that such dreams are by no means limited to believers in reincarnation: "The people to whom events of this kind happen come from all walks of life, all social backgrounds, and all ages. There is nothing specific about them, nothing that would single them out as being prone to reincarnation memories or even to psychic phenomena."[2]

Holzer cites the case of a California housewife named Juanita Thomson. At the age of ten Thomson had an unusually vivid dream that she was a woman who had lived in a small town somewhere in rural America. As Thomson grew older, the dream kept recurring and was so richly detailed that she was able to render a drawing of the place, complete with road layout, placements of shops, and the way the town was situated amid the surrounding hills. When Thomson was eighteen years old and on a cross-country trip that took her through Zanesville, Ohio, she suddenly found herself swept with a powerful sense of déjà vu. Not only was Zanesville the town she had drawn as a child, but the first thought that suddenly and inexplicably entered her mind as she drove through was, "There are a lot more houses now."[3]

Although numerous researchers have reported similar occurrences, one of the first to realize that a past-life dream can actually be induced was New York Jungian analyst Erlo van Waveren. Early in their careers both van Waveren and his wife, New York psychotherapist Ann van Waveren, studied directly with Dr. Jung and after the war were frequent visitors at the Jung Institute in Zurich. It was at this time, when van Waveren was in his early forties, that he had a dream that God appeared to him and transported him to the world of the dead.

The dream left van Waveren profoundly shaken, but he realized it was his psyche's way of telling him that there was something about the mysteries of death which he was meant to explore, so, with the assistance of his wife, he entered a state of meditation to see what he could find out. To his surprise, as soon as he was deeply relaxed, his mind suddenly became filled with what appeared to be memories of a previous existence. Moreover, he found that he had no choice but to allow the information to come tumbling out of his mouth. He states,

> I found myself telling Ann the purpose of both my present and former life as naturally as if I had been gossiping over a cup of tea. . . . Because of this voice which spoke from rock bottom, I was firmly convinced that in my former life I had been a teacher of life's values and had returned to continue in that work. . . . With the catalytic curiosity of a true wife, Ann asked me naturally and oh, so calmly, "But have you any idea who you were?" And just as calmly "it" spoke right through me and said "Fenelon." I was stunned, and could have been knocked over with a feather.[4]

Van Waveren went on to discover that Fenelon was a French archbishop during the reign of Louis XIV, but he became so upset when he reexperienced the emotions and frustrations that Fenelon had not been able to resolve during his lifetime that he ended his meditation before feeling he had truly understood the import of his dream. Skeptical about his experience and the idea of reincarnation in general, but impressed by the power and emotional content of his vision, van Waveren decided to try another tack. That night, before he went to bed, he asked his psyche to explain what it was attempting to communicate to him by providing him with another dream. He was not disappointed.

As he wrote in his [1978] book *Pilgrimage to the Rebirth*, that night he had a dream that he was in a hall of justice and that he was [a man] trying to break off an engagement with his new fiancée. However, the judge refused to grant his request and told him it was a marriage that must take place. Van Waveren awoke with a start and realized immediately that his unconscious was telling him that his rational side had to accept the new alliance it had formed with that portion of his psyche which contained his past-life memories.

Indeed, his unconscious had told him more than that. In the dream the judge had raised his right arm and revealed that there were nine glistening diamonds floating in the air. Van Waveren realized that his dreaming self was telling him that not one, but nine marriages were going to take place—he had nine previous lives with which he was going to have to become reacquainted. As promised, in the weeks that followed van Waveren's psyche went on to provide him with a series of dreams about his former incarnations.[5]

How to Recognize a Past-Life Dream

Frequently something about a dream will immediately tell you that it refers to one of your former lives. For example, in a study of past-life dreams, psychologist Frederick Lenz of the New School for Social Research in New York City found that many subjects were instantly swept with the awareness that what they were dreaming was a scene out of one of their former existences. In his book *Lifetimes*, he cites observations made by Pamela Cohen, a Montreal hospital worker who has had many past-life dreams, as typical of such experiences. Cohen states, "Dreams of my past lives are much clearer and more vivid than my regular dreams. They tell me things that help me understand certain feelings I have about things. Normally when I dream I'm not aware that I am dreaming. It's something I'm caught up in. But in these dreams I was fully aware the whole time that I was seeing into my past.''[6]

Another indication that a dream may be a past-life memory is if you find yourself wearing clothing from some other culture or age, or if you find that you are a completely different person or even a different sex in your dream than you are in your waking state. Even just noticing that other people around you are wearing clothing from a different era may indicate a reincarnational dream. Of course, such dreams may also have other meanings, but you should keep a record of them in your journal and view them as potential pieces of past-life information.

One final indication that a dream may contain past-life information is if it has an unusually powerful feeling of reality about it, or if it doesn't seem to have anything to do with your waking life, but still has such an impact on you that you aren't able to forget it. Past-life therapists have found that recurring dreams are especially good candidates. This does not mean that every recurrent dream you have is a past-life dream, or that past-life information cannot surface in single dreams, but if you find that you do have a recurrent dream that has troubled you for months or even years, you might examine it closely for possible past-life information.

What Do Spontaneous Past-Life Dreams Mean?

As van Waveren's experience suggests, a past-life dream is often the first way the unconscious starts to unfold a past-life memory (or series of past-life memories) to an individual. One reason for this is that the dreaming mind is less resistant to such information than the waking mind. Dreaming also seems to be one of the more gentle ways the inner self uses to prepare the waking self for a particular piece of past-life information, and therapists often find that patients begin to dream abut a particular past-life memory as a prelude to confronting it in a more conscious state, or even in other states of past-life awareness such as a hypnotic trance.

Similarly, spontaneous past-life dreams are often the unconscious mind's way of sending a telegram to the waking self and telling it that there is some past-life information that it might benefit from knowing. As Clyde Reid, a Boulder, Colorado, past-life therapist, has noted in his book *Dreams: Discovering Your Inner Teacher*,[7] many dreams are invitations calling us to deeper dialogues with the unconscious, but past-life dreams are especially significant. He states, "I am convinced that most past-life episodes that come up in our dreams are invitations to further work. They invite us to deal with that life or that memory by showing us a portion of the experience."[8]

Remembering Your Dreams

Before you can learn how to induce a past-life dream, you must first be able to remember your dreams. For some individuals this is second nature, but for others it is a talent that takes a bit of practice. If you find that you are a person who rarely remembers your dreams—or fear that you never dream at all—don't become discouraged. Numerous studies have shown that virtually everyone dreams, and as long as you are dedicated and willing to make an effort, dream recall is a relatively simple ability to acquire.

Keep a Dream Journal

One of the best ways to teach your mind to remember your dreams is to keep a dream journal. Keeping such a journal serves several purposes. First, it communicates to your unconscious mind that you are serious about remembering your dreams. Part of the reason many people forget their dreams is that they have never communicated to their inner selves that they want to remember them.

Keeping a dream journal also gives your dream memory the regular workout it needs in order to be able to remember. Remembering dreams is like doing push-ups. You must practice in order to be able to perform the task with any regularity, and if you stop for a while, you may have to start all over again to get the ability back.

Lastly, by dating and keeping a record of your dreams you will be able to perceive patterns and recurring themes more clearly that you might otherwise miss.

You can set aside part of your past-life journal as a dream diary, or you can keep a separate notebook or folder for your dreams and record only those that contain potential reincarnational memories in your past-life journal. Keep the journal by your bedside along with a pen and a convenient light source. If you find it easier, an alternative is to keep a small tape recorder by your bed and record each as you remember it. Then, at a more convenient time you can transfer your dictations to your dream journal.

Dream Technique Number 1—Basic Meditation

Step 1—Clear your body of all drugs that cause drowsiness It is important not to consume any alcohol or drugs that cause drowsiness during the day, because both tend to inhibit dream recall. If you are a regular consumer of alcohol, sleeping pills, or other drugs that affect the quality of sleep, you may have to go without them for several days before your system has cleaned itself out enough for you to be able to recall your dreams. Remember, of course, that you shouldn't suspend taking any prescription medications without first consulting your physician.

Step 2—Start to relax by emptying your mind and slowing your rate of breathing After you are comfortably in bed, empty your mind of all extraneous thoughts and start to relax by regulating your breathing. Breathe in and out in long, slow breaths. Focus for a few moments on keeping your breathing as deep, unstrained, and relaxed as possible. Many schools of thought—both ancient and modern—have shown that the rate at which you breathe sets the pace for your entire physical/emotional system. It is, in a sense, the orchestra conductor which sets the tempo for your meditative experience, and your breathing rate must remain slow, steady, and unstrained if you are to enter a state of relaxation.

Step 3—Tell yourself that all of your daily concerns and worries are leaving you Tell yourself, either mentally or aloud, that your mind is now uncluttered and very much at peace and that no extraneous thoughts will disturb you as you continue your relaxation.

Step 4—Talk to each part of your body and tell it to relax Begin by focusing on your toes. Tell them either mentally or aloud that they are completely relaxed and that all tension and muscle aches and pains are seeping out of them. Continue to breathe in slow, steady, and unstrained exhalations as you imagine your toes becoming so relaxed that you can barely feel them. Once this is accomplished, do the same thing with the rest of your feet. Continue the process with your lower legs, upper legs, buttocks, abdomen, hands, forearms, upper arms, back, and neck. Finally, tell yourself that your entire body is now so completely relaxed that all you are aware of is your head and that it, too, is so relaxed and at peace it feels like it is floating on a beautiful bed of clouds.

Step 5—Tell yourself that you are going to remember your dreams Once you have relaxed, say aloud, "Tonight I am going to remember my dreams." Or, "Tonight I am going to wake up after each one of my dreams." Don't just mouth the words, but concentrate on their meaning and meditate on your intention for several minutes before falling asleep. For best results it is important that you try to have this phrase be your last thought before drifting off to sleep (given your state of deep relaxation, this shouldn't be too difficult). Otherwise, if you perform the procedure and then allow your active mind to kick in again with all of your thoughts, worries, and concerns about your daily life, the technique will not be as effective.

Whether you are trying to remember your dreams or not, you should always use some technique to relax before you fall asleep because your last thoughts tend to determine and program the quality of your sleep. If you are worried about something or your mind is racing a mile a minute as you drift off into unconsciousness, your sleep will be tense and restless, and you will be much more prone to anxiety dreams than if you relax before sleeping.

Just before getting into bed, you might also spend a moment writing the evening's date in your dream journal. This will cue your unconscious mind still further that you want to remember your dream.

Step 6—Record any dreams you remember immediately on awakening It is important that you record your dreams the moment you wake up from them because dreams have a tendency to fade into a fog of forgetfulness if you do not immediately pay attention to them. As Cambridge, Massachusetts, psychiatrist Dr. Richard Goldwater observes, dreams are "like faeries. If you leave them goodies and treat them well, you can dance with them; if you don't deal with them well, they'll ignore you. They won't come around unless you create a hospitable place for them."[9]

Many people are able to remember their dreams right away by using this method. However, if you have any problem, here are some further techniques for you to try.

Dream Technique Number 2— The Alarm Clock Method

If you are an unusually heavy sleeper you may find it necessary to set an alarm clock for various intervals during the night. Or, if you prefer, set it for an hour or two before you have to get up and then keep setting it at half-hour intervals. The purpose of this is to try to have the alarm clock wake you up while you are in the middle of a dream. When this happens, quickly go over the details of the dream in your mind, and then record the dream in your dream journal or on a tape recorder. After relying on an alarm clock for a while, you will eventually teach your mind to remember dreams on its own.

Dream Technique Number 3— Nutrients That Encourage Dream Recall

There are several nutrients that encourage dream recall in some people. One is the essential amino acid phenylalanine that is found naturally in high-protein foods such as meat, cheese, and milk. Phenylalanine is one of the two amino acids found in the nonsugar sweetener aspartame (currently marketed as NutraSweet). Studies show that taking phenylalanine in its pure form on an empty stomach before retiring can reduce the amount of sleep an individual requires. I have found that, because it produces a lighter sleep, it can also greatly enhance dream recall.

In health food stores, phenylalanine is available in two forms, D- and L-phenylalanine. I have found that 250 to 1,000 milligrams of L-phenylalanine taken on an empty stomach before retiring lead to a night of vivid dreaming. However, this effect appears to be temporary, and L-phenylalanine may stop working for you after a few nights. Phenylalanine also has some potential side effects that must be taken into consideration. In doses larger than 500 milligrams it can cause headaches and insomnia in some people, and it should *never* be used by individuals with high blood pressure or a rare condition known as phenylketonuria. As with all vitamin and nonvitamin nutrients, to be on the safe side, always consult a physician before adding them to your dietary regimen.

Another nutrient that is said to enhance the dreaming process (although it has never had this effect on me) is vitamin B_{12}. B_{12} has no known toxicity and is found naturally in liver, yogurt, buttermilk, and most cheeses. I first learned of its dream-enhancing effects in Durk Pearson and Sandy Shaw's book *Life Extension*:

> [Vitamin B_{12}] can cause spectacular intensification of colors in dreams or sometimes even produce colors in dreams

of people who never before had colored dreams! It works about half the time in the small group of people we know who've tried it (sometimes the colors are so vivid they can wake you up!) A dose of 1,000 micrograms or so is effective. Take it *just* as you get into bed to sleep. If you take the B_{12} half an hour before bed, the dream-enhancing effect rarely works. Tolerance to this vitamin effect on dreams develops rapidly. So if you use large doses of B_{12} every day, it is rather unlikely that this effect will occur.[10]

Again, although B_{12} is an extremely safe vitamin and has no known toxic side effects, it is best to consult your physician before taking it in the relatively large dosages required to enhance dreaming.

Dream Technique Number 4—Discuss Your Dreams with Your Family and Friends

Another way to encourage dream recall is to discuss your dreams on a regular basis with some interested family member, a friend, or even in a dream discussion group.

One of the most striking examples that talking about dreams enhances recall can be found in the dreaming practices of an isolated jungle tribe known as the Senoi, who live in the rain forests of the Malay Peninsula. Although many people in the so-called modern world may have difficulty remembering their dreams, the Senoi have no problem whatsoever recalling all the myriad details of their nightly journeys through dreamland. This appears to be due in large part to the fact that not only do the Senoi value their dreams as important sources of knowledge and guidance, but every morning on awakening the entire family gathers together to discuss their dreams.[11]

The Senoi do more than just talk about their dreams. They also exert a good deal of control over them and work out many of their emotional and interpersonal problems in the medium of the dreamscape. For example, if a Senoi child tells his parents that he dreamed he was being chased by a tiger, the parents gently instruct the child that when he goes to bed the following night, he must dream that he is being chased by a tiger again, only this time he will turn and attack the tiger, causing it to vanish. Similarly, if a Senoi dreams that he has been attacked or affronted by a friend, he must go to the friend the following day and discuss the dream, making sure that any hidden animosities are worked out.

Scientists who have studied the Senoi point out that their dreaming techniques seem to work, for the Senoi live in a culture that has no violent crime or armed conflict, and virtually no mental and physical disease. The American anthropologist and psychologist, Kilton Stewart, who spent several years living among the Senoi, concluded that "they have built a system of inter-personal relations which, in the field of psychology, is perhaps on a level with our attainment in such areas as television and nuclear physics."[12]

Many modern dream researchers now believe that the Senoi have much to teach us, and conclude that studying, thinking about, and talking about dreams enhance dream recall for two reasons. First, they are other ways of communicating to your unconscious mind that you want dreams to become an important part of your daily life. Second, because we tend to dream about the things that we spend a lot of time thinking about, talking about dreams has a feedback effect that enriches the entire dreaming process.

Training Yourself to Dream About Past Lives

Once you are able to remember your dreams, you are ready to start programming them to tell you about your past lives. Many people are surprised to discover that programming a dream or getting a dream to answer a particular question is a remarkably easy process. It is also a very ancient practice. In her book *Creative Dreaming*, psychologist and dream researcher, Dr. Patricia Garfield, notes that techniques for programming dreams to answer specific questions have been found in Egyptian records dating from 3000 B.C. The ancient Assyrians called the practice *istiqara*, and among the ancient Greeks it was known as "dream incubation."[13]

Many modern researchers have also developed methods for "incubating" dreams. Although devoid of the mythological jargon that accompanied ancient techniques, the essence of these techniques remain the same. Inducing a dream about one of your past lives (or about any matter on which you desire dream guidance) involves three basic steps.

Step 1 After you have performed your nightly dream relaxation technique, spend some time thinking about what you want the dream to tell you and consider carefully the various possible answers you may receive. For example, you may want the dream to show you a past-life scene that you would like to become reacquainted with. Or you may want a dream that will show you an undiscovered past-life talent.

Step 2 Once you know what you want the dream to tell you, formulate your request in one clear and simple statement. You should always be careful to tell your unconscious mind that you do not wish to unearth any past-life memories that will be too traumatic or painful for you to deal with. Once I made the error of asking a dream to tell me about a particular past-life injury without adding this qualifier and found myself tossing and turning for a week with vivid nightmares of how I had died during a 12th-century Persian war.

Because of this possibility, you may also want to consult a pendulum (see p. 47) before asking a particular question, and then you can ask if your chosen subject is a safe one for you to dream about. Or you can simply couch your question in a way that will rule out a too-painful answer. For example, such a request might be phrased: "Tonight I would like to dream about an unpainful past life in which I knew my current husband." Or, "Tonight I would like to dream about an unpainful past life which explains my current religious concerns."

Step 3 On retiring, after you have placed yourself in a state of relaxation, repeat the request several times aloud and focus on it as you drift off to sleep.

The next morning when you awake—or during the night if you wake following a dream—write down any dream experiences that you have had, no matter how cryptic. Remember that although many past-life dreams will be clear and straightforward, a few, like van Waveren's dream about the judge with the nine diamonds suspended beneath his arm, will be expressed in the sometimes daunting symbolic language of the unconscious. If, following the dream-inducing exercise you have a vivid or moving dream, but at first it does not seem to pertain to your question, meditate upon it and let it incubate in your conscious mind. Look beneath its literal level and try to determine whether it has any allegorical meaning. If you still cannot figure out what it means, ask your dreaming self for further guidance.

After trying the above exercise, if you do not have immediate success, try it again, making sure that when you ask for a particular dream you are completely relaxed and are indeed focusing your thoughts intently on your request. If you still do not have success, try modifying the exercise in some way. For example, before going to bed, spend some time thinking about why you are asking that particular question, and what you might gain by knowing the answer. Even write a paragraph or two in your dream journal about your expectations. By spending this time focusing consciously on your request, you will increase the likelihood of impressing your desire in your unconscious mind.

Before going to bed, you might even spend some time imagining that you arc already in the midst of your requested dream and actually visualizing what you expect to see. If you do not know what to expect visually from a requested past-life dream, imagine instead the emotions you anticipate experiencing, and be sure to emphasize positive reactions, such as feelings of calm, increased understanding, and joy.

Do not expect all past-life dream experiences to be visual reenactments or even symbolic scenes. After programming myself to have a past-life dream, I have had dreams that contained no visual scenes at all, but consisted entirely of auditory experiences in the form of disembodied voices telling me the answers to my questions. I've also had dreams in which I was presented the information in written form. For example, a few years back I met a well-known Jamaican actress. The moment we were introduced, we were both swept with a powerful feeling of familiarity, a sense that we had known each other for a long, long time. We became instant good friends, and although we didn't discuss it at the time, we later learned that we both shared a conviction that we had known each other in a previous life.

About two years after our meeting a talented psychic was giving me a reading and suddenly started to describe my actress friend in detail—her life-style, emotional temperament, physical appearance—everything. He even described the nature of our friendship, the subjects we tended to talk about, and the things we shared in common; then he told me that the first time we were friends was in a life in the 1700s in a French fort somewhere in what is now the eastern United States. He also told me many other things that seemed to shed new light on the nature and intricacies of our current friendship.

My curiosity piqued, I decided to program a dream to see if it could tell me more about this revelation, and that evening while I slept, I had a dream that I was flying through a universe that was filled with nothing but an ocean of words, all suspended motionless in space. The firmament of this cosmos of words was not dark, but white, so that all of the floating words stood out sharply, and as I zoomed through this three-dimensional dictionary, I suddenly approached one word that filled my entire screen of vision, *Onondaga*. I did not know what the word meant at the time, but I wrote it down in my dream journal. When I researched the matter the next day, I found that Onondaga is the name of a lake in Syracuse, New York, and it was the site of Fort St. Marie de Gannentaha, an old French post and one of the area's first settlements.

How to Continue a Dream Once You Are Awake

If you have a past-life dream but do not understand what it is telling you, you have several options. You can simply make a note of it in your past-life journal and wait until further information turns up that helps you make sense of it. You can request further information to come through your dreams. You can use the dream as the subject of a past-life meditation, or you can continue the dream once you are awake by employing a technique devised by Jung and known as "active imagination."

In active imagination a person is completely awake but enters a relaxed state and then visualizes an evocative image or scene from a dream that he desires to know more about. Then, without any conscious interference, the visualizer simply allows the dream image to do what it will, growing and changing in whatever way its own internal processes dictate. Active imagining is a sort of conscious form of dreaming. Or, as British psychiatrist Anthony Storr puts it, it is "a state of reverie in which judgment [is] suspended but consciousness preserved."[14]

To continue a dream by employing active imagination, set aside approximately half an hour. Find a comfortable place and enter a state of relaxation. Once you have quieted your thoughts and feel completely relaxed, visualize the past-life dream you wish to explore further, and once again conjure up every detail you remember about the dream. You might also want to have a tape recorder present so that you do not have to interrupt your active imagining process by taking notes. Then, once you have as vivid a re-creation of the dream image as you can muster, simply sit back and allow the image to do whatever it wants. Remember also to follow your impulses.

For example, if you are visualizing the image of an 18th-century Austrian ballroom and you find that you suddenly have an urge to go through a doorway at the opposite end of the room, allow your imaginary self to go through the doorway. However, don't consciously try to anticipate what you are going to find there. Just sit back and allow your imagination to roam freely in any direction that it wishes. Similarly, don't be concerned if the ballroom suddenly becomes a boat, or if some inanimate object like a statue or a grandfather clock starts talking to you or giving you advice. Remember always that the language of inner experience is a symbolic one.

Jung also encouraged his patients to draw and paint their active imaginings, and this is another approach that you might try.

Once you have actively imagined a sequence of scenes or impressions, study them and see if any particular themes or messages pop out at you. Just as with dreams, do not automatically assume that the information you glean from active imagining is a literal transcript of one of your past lives. It may be, or it may be a symbolic message from your unconscious, or even a stream of allegorical images pertaining to a range of psychological events taking place in your mind. Whatever the case, concentrate on the scene or image that strikes you as the most meaningful and see what its overall message is telling you. If you find, for example, you see an image of many people starving, examine yourself and see if your unconscious mind is actually trying to tell you that there is some part of you that is starving. Similarly, if you see an image of Marilyn Monroe, do not automatically assume that you have some sort of past-life association with Marilyn Monroe. Instead, ask yourself what Marilyn Monroe represents to you on an archetypal or symbolic level, and see if that image helps you unravel the message your unconscious is giving you. Once you feel that you have deciphered such a sequence of images, write them down in your past-life journal as another possible area wiped off your past-life fresco.

In addition to being a tool for unraveling past-life dreams, active imagination has many other applications as well. Jung encouraged his patients to use it as a way of establishing a consistent and continuing dialogue with their unconscious minds—an ongoing process that Jung felt was a vital part of every human being's daily life.[15]

Lucid Dreaming

Another dreaming technique that can be used to unearth past-life information, but which is more difficult to master, is "lucid dreaming," or the ability to be awake in one's dreams. In a lucid dream, not only are you completely conscious of the fact that you are dreaming, but you can also use that awareness to direct and control the subject matter of the dream. I have only been able to program myself to have a few past-life lucid dreams, but I count them among the most profound experiences in my life. Thus, in spite of the difficulty of mastering the ability, lucid dreaming is still a method worth exploring.

Like many of the techniques offered in this book, lucid dreaming is a very ancient practice. In Tibet the ability to be awake in one's dreams was considered prerequisite to spiritual advancement and was known as the Yoga of the Dream State or *Mi-lam*. In his book *The Tantric Mysticism of Tibet*, the distinguished Orientalist and translator of the *I Ching* John Blofeld states, "In this yoga, the adept is taught to enter the dream state at will, to explore its characteristics and return to the waking state without any break in his stream of normal consciousness. Thereby he discovers the illusory nature of both states and learns how to die . . . and to be reborn without loss of memory."[16]

Although researchers in the Western world have been studying lucid dreaming for at least a century, it has only been in the past several years that this curious mental state has really come into its own among members of the scientific community. In 1981 the Association for the Psychophysiological Study of Sleep acknowledged lucid dreaming as a phenomenon worthy of scientific scrutiny by allowing a number of papers to be presented on the subject, and since then increasing numbers of researchers have been drawn to it.[17]

Techniques for Inducing Lucid Dreams

Before you can learn how to induce a past-life lucid dream, it is first necessary to learn how to have lucid dreams in general. After learning how to remember your dreams, one technique is simply to request a lucid dream during your nightly dream-programming session. This can be accomplished by telling yourself, "Tonight while I am dreaming, I am going to realize that I am dreaming." As with all dream requests, this sentence should be meditated upon and repeated several times with conviction.

In his book *Lucid Dreaming*—an excellent sourcebook on both the history and current scientific status of lucid dreaming—Stanford University psychologist Stephen LaBerge offers an alternative method that he arrived at as the result of his research at the Stanford University Sleep Laboratory. LaBerge, one of the modern pioneers in lucid dreaming research, calls his method the Mnemonic Induction of Lucid Dreams or MILD. In spite of its somewhat intimidating name, LaBerge notes that MILD is based on nothing more complex or esoteric "than our ability to remember that there are actions we wish to perform in the future."[18] After stressing that a powerful desire to have a lucid dream is essential, LaBerge outlines the procedure in four simple steps.

1. At some point in the early morning when you have awakened spontaneously from a dream, quickly go over every detail of the dream in your mind and repeat the process several times until you have completely memorized the dream.

2. Then, while you are still lying in bed, repeat to yourself several times, "Next time I'm dreaming, I want to remember to recognize that I'm dreaming."

3. After repeating this phrase, picture yourself back in the dream you just finished dreaming, only imagining that this time you realize that you are dreaming.

4. Keep the visualization in your mind until it is clearly fixed or you fall back asleep.[19]

If all goes well, LaBerge asserts that by following this procedure you will find yourself lucid in another dream (although not necessarily one that resembles the previous dream).

German psychologist Paul Tholey suggests that you can induce lucid dreams simply by getting into the habit of asking yourself, "Am I dreaming?" five or ten times a day. By habitually asking yourself whether you are dreaming during your waking hours, you greatly increase the likelihood that you will ask yourself the same question while you are dreaming, and by adhering to this procedure, Tholey asserts that most people will have a lucid dream within a month.[20]

One trick I use to help me stick to this regimen is to write the question on little note cards and place the cards in various places I glance at often during the day. For example, you can place a card on the mirror in the bathroom cabinet where you'll see it when you brush your teeth, above the sink where you do dishes, on your desk or in a desk drawer that you open and shut frequently, on a nightstand, on a bookmark, on a frequently used notebook and, if you are inventive, you might even want to tape a small reminder of some sort somewhere on the face of your watch.

Tholey's suggestion is not new. In his book *Teachings of Tibetan Yoga*, the Buddhist scholar Garma C. C. Chang cites a passage from an 11th-century Tibetan manuscript that offers a similar technique for inducing a lucid dream. After first advising the adept to cultivate a powerful desire to become conscious in the dream state, and to stay away from intoxicants and other substances that pollute the body, the manuscript states, "To think continuously in the daytime that all one sees, hears, touches . . . is in a dream, will greatly increase one's chances of recognizing dreams at night."[21]

Although not couched in the form of a question, the end result of such an exercise—constantly reinforcing an introspective attitude toward the possible dreamlike nature of an experience—remains the same.

In his now famous series of books detailing his conversations with a Yaqui Indian *brujo* or sorcerer named don Juan, the anthropologist Carlos Castaneda reports that the Yaqui

Indians also speak of a special type of "dreaming" that bears a striking resemblance to lucid dreaming. As don Juan informed Castaneda, " 'Dreaming' entailed cultivating a peculiar control over one's dreams to the extent that the experiences undergone in them and those lived in one's waking hours acquired the same pragmatic valence. The sorcerers' allegation was that under the impact of 'dreaming' the ordinary criteria to differentiate a dream from reality became imperative."[22]

The technique don Juan taught Castaneda to use to achieve such a lucid state was to associate constantly looking at his hands with realizing that he was dreaming. The point was, of course, that by inextricably linking the two activities together in his mind, sooner or later Castaneda would glance at his hands in a dream and trigger the same realization. Castaneda reports that although acquiring lucidity in a dreaming state was difficult to master, he eventually became successful by employing this method.

What to Do if You Have Problems

For some people, lucid dreaming is a relatively easy talent to acquire, but for most it takes practice. If you try lucid dreaming but have no success, there are several things you can do. One is to set your alarm for very early in the morning and perform a lucidity-programming meditation then. Research has shown that lucid dreaming is a much easier state to attain after several hours of sleep, and most lucid dreams occur in the early morning.

For those who are having difficulty, Garfield suggests thinking more about dreams during the day, concentrating on trying to recognize what sort of rules distinguish your waking experiences from those you have come to expect in your dreams.[23] Again, because we are prone to dreaming abut what occupies our waking thoughts, this practice has a tendency to heighten dream awareness during sleep.

The 11th-century Tibetan manuscript cited by Chang asserts that if a person is still not successful after many attempts, this is an indication that "his mind is full of distracting thoughts, or his yearning to do so is weak," and these two problems must be remedied before success can be expected.[24]

How to Induce a Past-Life Lucid Dream

Although there is little modern research connecting the lucid-dreaming state to past-life recall, researchers agree that you can choose and direct virtually anything you wish to occur in a lucid dream, so past-life recall is not precluded. In my own past-life lucid dreams I have employed various techniques.

For example, in one, on finding myself awake and in the midst of a lucid dream, I merely willed myself to go back to a past-life scene and found myself whisked back through time on a vivid past-life memory experience.

In another, on awakening in the dream I found myself in the presence of another individual, an indistinct but human-shaped energy presence that emanated a feeling of great wisdom and compassion, and I asked this entity to show me one of my past lives. At this request the entity took me by the hand and literally flew me through the clouds and back through time. It then proceeded to explain to me what I was seeing and answered my questions as we visited a scene from one of my previous incarnations. (See pages 81–3 for more about the role of such "guides" or "guardian figures" in past-life experiences in general.)

The key to turning a lucid dream into past-life lucid dream thus appears to be simply to will it to happen. However, if you find yourself in a lucid state, it is very important that you keep your thoughts positive and focused. In one lucid dream experience, while I was flying over a beautiful mountain lake, I suddenly became frightened at the realization that all I had to do was imagine a sea serpent beneath the waters of the lake, and one would materialize. Sure enough, as soon as this thought passed through my mind, a sea serpent started to materialize in the depths of the sparkling clear waters, and like a dutiful Senoi child, I had to suppress my fear quickly and will the sea serpent to vanish before I could continue.

The lesson inherent in this is that during a past-life lucid dream you should always be on your guard to keep extraneous thoughts and impulses from steering the dream off in other directions. I feel that it is important to point out that the only time I have not encountered this danger during a past-life lucid dream is when I have been guided through the experience by the aforementioned guardian figures. Other researchers have also commented on the apparent importance of such dream guides. For example, Garfield reports that, although it has not yet became a part of modern lucid dream research, the concept of conjuring up a protective guardian figure can be found in many older and culturally diverse schools of thought. Among the native Americans such "dream friends" were essential before the seeker could undertake extensive journeys through the world of dreams. The Ojibwa referred to them as *manidos* ("guardian spirits").[25] In Tibet they were referred to as *viras* ("heroes") and *dakinis* ("fairies"), and every adept was advised to make friends with one of several before traveling deeper into the varied planes of the dream state.[26] The Senoi call them simply "father" or "child-friend," and although every Senoi dreamer cultivates at least one or two, those who are lucky enough to make the acquaintance of many such guardian figures are considered to be great shamans. It is intriguing to note that the Senoi believe that a guardian figure need not be human in appearance to provide such protection but can be equally effective even if it assumes the shape of a natural object such as a rock or flower.[27]

Thus, once you have reached the point where you can induce your own past-life lucid dream, instead of venturing off on your own, you may always want to conjure up a guide or dream friend to assist you. The kinds of image you might visualize as a dream friend and what such guardian figures represent are both topics that will be discussed in the next chapter.

Endnotes

1. D. Scott Rogo, *The Search for Yesterday* (Englewood Cliffs, New Jersey; Prentice-Hall, 1985), pp. 27–28.

2. Hans Holzer, *Life Beyond Life* (West Nyack, New York: Parker Publishing, 1985), pp. 27–28.

3. Ibid., p. 31.

4. Erlo van Waveren, *Pilgrimage to the Rebirth* (New York: Samuel Weiser, 1978), pp. 19–20.

5. Ibid., pp. 21–22.

6. Frederick Lenz, Ph.D., *Lifetimes* (New York: Fawcett, 1979), p. 33.

7. Clyde H. Reid, *Dreams: Discovering Your Inner Teacher* (Pennsylvania: Winston Press, 1983).

8. Clyde H. Reid, "Dreams and Past Lives," *The Association for Past-Life Research and Therapy Newsletter* 5, no. 2, Spring 1985): 4.

9. Marc Barasch, "A Hitchhiker's Guide to Dreamland," *New Age* (October 1983): 41.

10. Durk Pearson and Sandy Shaw, *Life Extension* (New York: Warner Books, 1982), p. 195.

11. Kilton Stewart, "Dream Theory in Malaya," in *Altered States of Consciousness*, ed. Charles T. Tart (New York: John Wiley & Sons, 1969), pp. 159–68; see also Patricia Garfield, Ph.D., *Creative Dreaming* (New York: Ballantine, 1974), pp. 80–117.

12. Stewart, "Dream Theory," pp. 160–61.

13. Garfield, *Creative Dreaming*, p. 26; see also p. 20.

14. C. G. Jung, *The Essential Jung*, selected and introduced by Anthony Storr (Princeton, New Jersey: Princeton University Press, 1983), p. 21.

15. Janet Dallett, "Active Imagination in Practice," in *Jungian Analysis*, ed. Murray Stein (Boulder, Colorado: Shambhala, 1982), p. 172.

16. John Blofeld, *The Tantric Mysticism of Tibet* (New York: E. P. Dutton, 1977), p. 232.

17. Stephen LaBerge, Ph.D., *Lucid Dreaming* (Los Angeles: J. P. Tarcher, 1985), pp. 70–71.

18. Ibid., p. 140.

19. Ibid., pp. 140-41.

20. Paul Tholey, "Techniques for Inducing and Maintaining Lucid Dreams," *Perceptual and Motor Skills* 57 (1983): 79–80, as quoted in LaBerge, *Lucid Dreaming*, p. 132.

21. Garma C. C. Chang, trans. and ed., *Teachings of Tibetan Yoga* (Secaucus, New Jersey: Citadel, 1974), p. 88.

22. Carlos Castaneda, *Tales of Power* (New York: Simon & Schuster, 1974), p. 18.

23. Garfield, *Creative Dreaming*, p. 149.

24. Chang, *Tibetan Yoga*, p. 67.

25. Garfield, *Creative Dreaming*, p. 67.

26. Ibid., p. 157.

27. Ibid., p. 91.

4 ~

Meditation Techniques

> For various reasons meditation—accompanied by a life of altruism and service—may ultimately prove to be the best path to self-knowledge and knowledge of one's past existences. Properly done, meditation carries with it the greatest spiritual and psychological safeguards. In this method the memories are not forced to the surface, nor is the knowledge of them likely to come prematurely. Their intimacy is preserved and their import is not likely to be misunderstood by an alien, though sympathctic, viewer.
>
> GINA CERMINARA, *Many Lives, Many Loves*

Once you have learned to make past-life information surface in your dreams, with a little practice you can also encourage it to surface while you are awake. One of the most commonly used techniques for doing this is meditation.

The use of meditation to unlock memories of past lives is by no means new. As early as the 4th century B.C., Patanjali, the founder of Yoga philosophy, was telling his students that they could remember their previous births simply by engaging in meditation.[1] Similarly, in the *Itivuttaka*, an ancient Buddhist text, it is written that through devotion to meditation one can recollect "many a past existence with all its characteristic features and particulars," and be able to say, "There I have been and had such a name, belonged to such a family, had such an appearance, ate such kinds of food, partook of such pleasures and sufferings, and such was my lifespan."[2]

Safeguards to Establish Before Beginning Meditation

The only difference between ancient and modern meditation techniques is that most of the ancient ones assert that months, even years, of rigorous practice are required to achieve results. However, modern research has shown that recalling past-life memories through meditation is astonishingly easy, so easy, in fact, that many investigators warn past-life explorers not to let rapid success seduce them into blundering ahead recklessly without first establishing the proper safeguards.

Safeguard 1—Do Not Begin with an Attitude of Fear or Worry

For most people, exploring past lives through resonance or dreams is a relatively safe endeavor because both methods involve feelings and processes that they have experienced before. However, when you begin to delve into some of the more advanced techniques given in this book and start to bring your past-life memories to the surface more aggressively, you may find yourself swept with fears and apprehensions.

One fear that many people have is that they will unlock a memory which is too painful for them to deal with. Another is that they will stumble across a past life in which they were a shameful or disreputable individual. These are both possibilities, but as I pointed out in Chapter 1, as a rule, your unconscious mind will automatically protect you from memories that are too painful or traumatic for your conscious mind to deal with.

You can also help your unconscious mind perform this natural function by trusting in its ability to protect you and maintaining an attitude of peace and calm whenever you embark on any deep past-life explorations. Do not expect anything painful or bad to happen because such expectations can, in a sense, become self-fulfilling prophecies. Your unconscious mind takes things very literally, and if it constantly perceives that all of your requests for past-life information are colored by fear, it can sometimes mistakenly assume that you are actually requesting fearful information.

Safeguard 2—Proceed Cautiously and Listen to Your Own Inner Counsel

Although your unconscious mind will naturally try to protect you, you must do your part and pay attention to what it is telling you. Move slowly, and as memories start to surface, pay careful attention to what your own intuitive voice advises you to do next. If you start to unlock what seems to be an innocuous past-life memory, but you are suddenly filled with an inexplicable uneasiness or feeling of foreboding—*stop*. Either abandon probing that memory altogether, or ask your unconscious mind for advice on what to do next by employing a pendulum, finger movements, or by requesting that the information be given to you in a dream. But above all, do not just plow recklessly through the inner reaches of your psyche. Your psyche is a complex and multilayered entity, and you must treat it with both consideration and respect if you are to negotiate its labyrinthine passageways safely.

Safeguard 3—Actively Solicit the Advice of Your Unconscious Mind

Perhaps the most important point for you to keep in mind as you unravel your past lives is that your "true self"—the self that contains the totality of all your incarnations and which now lies hidden in your unconscious mind—is far vaster and more experienced than your current conceptions of yourself may allow. It is also intelligent and wise and waiting anxiously to share its wisdom with you, to help you blossom into the larger being that is both your birthright and your destiny.

Get into the habit of communicating with this larger and wiser part of you by carrying on a regular dialogue with your unconscious mind. Consult your unconscious mind, not only about possible painful or traumatic past-life memories, but about all decisions involving past-life explorations (or anything else in your life on which you seek advice). Again, use whatever technique is easiest for you—pendulum, finger movements, or dreams.

As you become more adept at communicating with your unconscious mind, you may find that you can eventually dispense with these procedures and communicate directly with your inner self. For example, you may find that you will reach a point at which you can mentally ask a question and your own intuitive voice will instantly tell you the answer. The truth is that the unconscious mind is always giving us pieces of advice and flashes of insight. The reason that we are generally unaware of this fact is that all too often we allow our minds to be so overrun with the ceaseless chatter of everyday thoughts that we do not pay attention to the ever-present whisperings of our unconscious. Nonetheless, you can do yourself no greater favor than to establish an ongoing line of communication with your unconscious mind, your vaster and wiser self.

Safeguard 4—Ask for Protection from a "Guardian Figure"

One of the most intriguing phenomena that surface during explorations of the human unconscious are the appearance of "guardian figures." These are angels, spirit guides, or cosmic teachers who protect the explorer and offer guidance during journeys through the landscape of the inner self. As we have seen, such figures surface often in dream explorations, but they are associated with numerous other phenomena having to do with the human psyche.

For example, people who have undergone "near-death experiences," or NDEs, frequently report that they were guided or watched over by some sort of protective and loving spiritual entity during their experience. In the field of transpersonal psychology (the branch of psychology that studies nonordinary or altered states of consciousness), encounters with spiritual or "suprahuman" entities are also frequently reported. Even individuals who routinely spend time in isolation tanks report encounters with such guides or teachers.

So it is not surprising that the spontaneous appearance of guardian figures also plays an important role in many past-life experiences. Past-life therapists have found that patients often report the presence of guides when they are regressed to states of past-life awareness. Such guides perform various functions. Sometimes they explain what is happening during a past-life experience or why a particular lifetime has been shown to an individual. Sometimes they are present merely to offer advice and moral support. Interestingly, researchers have found that when individuals are regressed to the interim between one past life and the next they often report that many spiritual teachers are present to counsel them and help them plan their next birth.

What are such beings? Some people prefer to view them simply as personified aspects of their own unconscious mind, similar to Freud's concept of the "super-ego." Others believe that they are actual spiritual entities existing on higher planes of consciousness. Whatever the explanation, many past-life therapists have found that such personages can be invaluable in guiding a subject to those memories which contain the most beneficial information. They can also help guide an individual away from memories that are too painful to explore safely. Because of the protective and positive function of these entities, some therapists refuse to regress a subject unless it is done under the guidance of a guardian figure. For example, California psychiatrist Dr. Ernest Pecci states, "I rarely perform a past-life regression unless my subject has successfully contacted a spiritual guide or teacher who represents a link to the Inner Mind and who can assume an important function in helping to direct the course of the therapy."[3]

Before you embark on a past-life meditation (or any of the other more advanced techniques that will be given in this book), you should first seek the advice and protection of a guardian figure. To do this, decide which of the explanations of guardian figures you feel the most comfortable with. For example, decide whether you prefer to view your own guardian figure(s) as:

- an expression of your super-ego or unconscious mind
- an actual spiritual entity or entities existing on a higher plane of consciousness or reality such as a guardian angel or a spirit guide
- a religious personage such as God, Jesus, or Buddha
- some other positive alternative that appeals to your own personal belief system—your higher self, or oversoul perhaps

Then, before each past-life exploration, spend a few minutes relaxing and visualizing the guardian figure you have chosen. If you feel that you do not know what the guardian figure you have chosen might look like, visualize him or her as a being composed entirely of a pure and brilliant white light. If this image still does not work for you, simply try to imagine what your guardian figure's presence might feel like. For instance, try to imagine the presence of a being whose only goal is to love, guide, and protect you. Then, once you feel that you have the image of your guardian figure in your mind—or sense its presence in some other way—recite the following out loud:

> Please [insert the name of your chosen guardian figure(s) here] guide and protect me as I now enter into my deeper self to explore who and what I have been in previous lives. Gently lead me to only those memories that I am ready to reexperience and which will teach me things that will help me grow and become a happier, healthier, and more fulfilled person in this life. Shield me from anything that it is too painful for me to reexperience and protect me from all things negative as I travel on my way. For this I offer you my blessings and thank you for your wisdom and loving protection.

If you wish, at this point you can also ask your guardian figure(s) to help guide you to the answer to any other questions that you have, such as: Why was a particular memory shown to me? What can I do to integrate the information I have learned into my everyday life? What can I do to heal some repeating karmic problem that I have learned about?

Always remember to thank your guardian figures for their assistance and treat them with reverence and respect. You should do this even if you view them as subcomponents of your own unconscious mind. The unconscious mind speaks in a language of symbols. By treating its symbolic emissaries with respect, you communicate to your psyche how you would like it to behave toward you.

Safeguard 5—Surround Yourself with a Protective White Light

In addition to calling upon the protection of a guardian figure, many therapists advise their subjects to surround themselves with a protective white light before entering states of past-life awareness. Again, like asking for protection from guardian figures, explanations vary for why such a process proves effective. Some say that it is simply another symbolic way of asking the unconscious mind for protection. Others believe that it actually surrounds the past-life explorer with a shield of psychic energy that protects one from harmful psychic influences. Whatever the explanation, the technique has a long and varied history and can be found in surprisingly disparate sources, from old books on occultism to modern texts on visualization techniques to help cancer patients to try to rid their bodies of illness.

To create such a shield you should close your eyes and enter a state of relaxation. Then visualize yourself as completely enclosed in a sphere or egg of radiant and protective white light. Imagine that even your breath is luminous and that each time you exhale you add to the power of the light. With each breath you take, keep visualizing the light getting stronger and stronger until it is so bright that you can scarcely look at it in your mind's eye. When it reaches this point, tell yourself either silently or aloud that you are now completely protected by an impenetrable barrier of light and that nothing untoward or evil can now harm you.

What You Need to Know About Meditation Before Beginning

Once you have familiarized yourself with the safety precautions that you should take, there are a few basics about meditation that you should know. In its simplest terms, meditation is the ability to relax and concentrate your attention on one thing to the exclusion of all else. To do this it will be necessary for you to master the ability to control and quiet the chatter of your everyday thoughts, to relax, and to completely dispel any physical or emotional tensions that you might have.

Although various techniques to accomplish these tasks will be given in this section, it is important that you keep in mind that there is no single correct way to meditate. If you find that one approach doesn't work, don't be afraid to mix-and-match techniques from various procedures to suit your own personal requirements. Similarly, don't be afraid to come up with your own techniques. Just as everyone prefers a different sleeping position and a different hardness or softness of mattress, everyone must also find their own approach to achieving a meditative state.

Creating the Right Atmosphere

Some people assume that they must be sitting in a lotus position in order to be able to meditate, but this is not the case. You may find that sitting in a lotus position helps you meditate, or you may find that you have better results if you sit in an easy chair or lie down on a couch. I personally prefer to lie on a carpeted floor when I meditate, but you should experiment and find the position that suits you best. One word of advice—many experts advise against trying to meditate while lying in bed because its association with sleep tends to make the mind bypass the meditative state and drift off to sleep.

You may also find that it is easier for you to meditate when there is a stick of incense burning. Or having an unobtrusive background sound, such as a recording of the ocean or a gentle summer rain, may help you relax. However, it is advisable to turn off the recording after you are in a meditative state, or the sound may unduly color your past-life impressions.

Refer to Chapter 1 for more ideas on creating the best setting for meditation.

Learning How to Meditate

If you have never meditated before, don't expect to be able to master it immediately. In a state of deep meditation you should feel incredibly peaceful, relaxed, and unworried. If you go through the steps of placing yourself in a meditative state, but find that you are still fidgety, tense, or concerned about something going on in your life, you have not yet accomplished your task.

Another indication that you still have some work ahead of you is if you find that your thoughts continually stray from the object of your meditation. For example, if after the first twenty seconds of a breathing exercise, you find yourself thinking about your finances or some other aspect of your worldly life, you have not yet learned to quiet your thoughts and enter a state of meditation. Don't be surprised if this happens, because learning how to keep your thoughts focused on one thing for an extended period of time is by no means as easy as it seems.

If you find that it is difficult for you to shut out the world and quiet the constant interruption of your own thoughts, don't become discouraged. In certain ways the mind is very much like a muscle, and just as you cannot run a marathon or play a piece by Chopin the first time out, it may take a bit of practice before you learn how to control your own thinking processes and keep your mind from perpetually carrying on a running conversation with itself.

As a preliminary exercise, spend a few moments a day staring at a candle flame, and try to think of nothing but the flame. Don't think of the flame in terms of words like "flame," "red," or "flickering," but try to contemplate it without using words. Think only of its essence and see how many seconds you can do this before a stray thought pops into your mind. When one does, push it back out and carry on with your contemplation. Start out by doing this for a few minutes a day, and keep it up until you can stare at the candle flame for ten minutes or longer without thinking of any other thoughts. When you are able to do this, you have developed your powers of concentration enough that you should have little trouble achieving a meditative state.

If you find that you still have difficulty quieting your thoughts, another exercise that you might try is to spend ten minutes or so continuously moving every muscle of your body. Stand up, move around, flex all of your fingers, wave your arms, jog in place, shake your head, make sounds with your mouth, and keep every muscle in your body as active and as busy as you can manage. Then, after you have done this for about ten minutes, stop suddenly and quickly lie down, pushing every extraneous thought out of your mind as you do so. Concentrate only on the sense of relief you feel at being able to stop, and on your breath as it flows in and out, but don't think of either of these things in terms of words or sentences. Simply *feel* them and see how long you can maintain your meditation.

Learning How to Visualize

Virtually all of the past-life meditative techniques that will be given in this book require that you be able to visualize certain objects and scenes very clearly in your mind's eye. If you find that you have difficulty doing this, your problem may be due to an inability to focus your concentration, so the meditation exercises will still apply. However, if you find that you can easily become very relaxed and quiet your thoughts, but have trouble conjuring up some of the required visual images, you may have to exercise your visualization muscles as well.

One way to do this is to make yourself comfortable in a quiet and dimly lit room. Then close your eyes and try to imagine what the room looks like without opening them. Slowly and carefully sketch every feature of the room in your mind's eye, and don't let the image be replaced by any other imaginings. If you have to, take a peek to see if you missed something, but then quickly close your eyes and continue with the procedure, making your mental image as real as possible and holding it for as long as you can.

As another exercise, imagine that you are gazing at a blackboard in a classroom, and you have a piece of chalk in your hand. Then, reach out and write a sentence on the blackboard, such as, "Mary had a little lamb." Try to feel the texture of the chalk in your hand and feel yourself writing with it. Watch every stroke and observe how you make each letter. When you have finished, step back and look at the entire sentence as you have written it on the blackboard. Approach the blackboard again, and write the next sentence of the nursery rhyme beneath the first, and then the next, filling the board with as many sentences as you can hold unwaveringly in your mind.

Once you have mastered these techniques, you are ready to go on and try an actual past-life meditation.

Basic Past-Life Meditation

Like most preparations for past-life meditations, the following instructions for a basic past-life meditation require an "induction image."

This is a scene that you will visualize during the course of the meditation and which will help you open the door to one of your past-life memories. In the following instructions I have used the induction image of a tunnel. However, there are many images that may be substituted in this basic meditation, and a list of some others, as well as their various pros and cons, will be given after the description of the basic technique.

Step 1—Choose a place to meditate Choose a place to meditate according to the guidelines discussed in Chapter 1.

Step 2—Start to relax by emptying your mind and slowing your rate of breathing As soon as you have settled into your meditation position, empty your mind of all extraneous thoughts and start to relax by regulating your breathing. Breathe in and out in long, slow, and steady breaths. Focus for a few moments on keeping your breathing as deep, unstrained, and relaxed as possible. As with the relaxation technique employed in the chapter on dreams, continue to maintain a slow and even breathing pace throughout the duration of your meditation.

Step 3—Tell yourself that all of your daily concerns and worries are leaving you Tell yourself that your mind is uncluttered and very much at peace, and that no intrusive thoughts will disturb you as you continue to go deeper and deeper into a state of relaxation.

Step 4—Talk to each part of your body and tell it to relax Begin by telling your toes, either mentally or aloud, that they are completely relaxed and that all tension, muscle aches, and pains are seeping out of them. Continue to breathe in slow, steady, and unstrained exhalations as you imagine your toes becoming so relaxed that you can barely feel them. Once this is accomplished do the same thing with the rest of your feet. Continue the process with your legs, lower arms, upper arms, back, and neck. Finally, tell yourself that your entire body is now so completely relaxed that all you are aware of is your head and that it, too, is so relaxed and at peace that it feels like it is floating on a beautiful bed of clouds.

Step 5—Tell your unconscious what you want to accomplish When you are in a deeply relaxed state, tell your unconscious mind what you hope to accomplish during your meditation. You should do this out loud, speaking in a slow, steady voice, and remembering that your unconscious mind takes everything literally. For example, you might ask your unconscious mind to show you a past-life memory that it would be beneficial for you to be aware of. Or you may have a more specific question such as, "Show me the life in which I first met my current husband." Or, "Tell me if a dream I keep having has any past-life significance." Or "Show me a past-life experience in which I learned something that will help me get through this crisis."

Step 6—Ask your inner self for protection Once you have outlined specific goals for yourself, remind your unconscious mind to show you only those memories that you will be able to experience without discomfort or anxiety. Again, it is important that you speak out loud when you do this. Tell your unconscious mind that if it must show you an unpleasant memory, it should do so in a way that is gentle and will not cause you any pain. Stress that you only want to know those things that you are ready to see and which will further the growth and happiness of all concerned.

At this point ask the guardian figure that you have chosen for yourself—your super-ego, oversoul, spirit guides, or religious entity—to watch over and protect you as you journey into your psyche. As you continue to breathe slowly and deeply, surround yourself with a circle of protective white light. Imagine that each exhalation of your breath is itself a luminous mist and adds to the light. Ask your guardian figure to see that the white light is maintained throughout your meditation, and that it protects you from all harmful influences, real or imagined.

Step 7—Enter an even deeper state of relaxation and then visualize yourself entering a tunnel, beyond which you will see one of your past lives Tell yourself now that at the count of five you are going to enter an even deeper state of relaxation. Then recite the following either mentally or aloud: "One . . . I am becoming more relaxed than I have ever been. Two . . . all cares and worries have now left me, and my body is so buoyant that it is floating on a bed of clouds. Three . . . at the count of five I will be deeply and completely relaxed . . . Four . . . Five."

As soon as you have reached five, imagine that your body has actually floated up from its bed of clouds. Imagine that you feel a gentle breeze and see the clouds swirling gracefully around you. As you continue to move through the clouds, imagine that you see a long tunnel before you, a tunnel composed entirely of beautiful swirling clouds. Because you are weightless, you are able to enter the cloud and walk along its misty surface. As you continue to walk, tell yourself that at the end of the tunnel you are going to witness a past-life scene or memory about yourself. Then imagine that you see the end of the tunnel coming into sight. As you continue to walk toward it, don't worry if you do not immediately see anything. Be completely at peace, and when you reach the end of the tunnel, quickly look down at your feet and see what they look like. Perhaps you will see them wearing leather sandals, or perhaps they will be bare. Look at your legs and see what sort of clothing you are wearing, and then look up at your surroundings.

If you don't see anything, don't worry. Be patient and, above all, don't try to force an image. You may instantly start to see a past-life scenario unfolding before you like a movie, or you may flash on a single image, a face, a domestic scene, or a house. Your unconscious mind will show you what it is necessary for you to see. It is important that you maintain an attitude of utter peace and calm as you simply sit back and let it lead the way.

Choosing a Different Induction Image

If you have practiced learning both how to relax and how to visualize, and have become skilled at the art of meditation, you will probably see at least a few past-life images your first time out. Indeed, many people see quite vivid and complex past-life scenarios the first time they try this technique. However, if you do not receive any past-life information initially, practice the technique a few times. Then, if you still have problems, try using a different induction image. For example, instead of visualizing a tunnel of swirling clouds, visualize a tunnel that is composed of some other material, such as a tunnel built out of a beautiful bower of trees. If the image of a tunnel does not work for you, you can also try some of the other popular induction images listed below.

Hallway Meditation

Imagine yourself walking down a long hallway, or down a long set of stairs with a door at the bottom. Some researchers suggest that the past-life explorer envision the hallway as being filled with many doors, each one opening onto a past-life memory. One visualization image that has proved quite effective for me is to imagine myself in a mansion in which each room contains one of my past lives. This image was first suggested to me by a dream I had, although the Biblical line "In my Father's house are many mansions"—a phrase that many have interpreted as alluding to reincarnation—adds a further veneer of meaning which may increase its appeal for you. Of course, your powers of concentration and visualization must be finely honed to be able to conjure up such an image at first, but once you get the hang of it, the imaginary surroundings you build around yourself will take on a life of their own.

Elevator Meditation

Another popular induction image is an elevator in which you are either ascending or descending (whichever you prefer) to one of your previous incarnations. Decide on which floor your past-life experience is going to take place and envision the floor indicator moving slowly until you reach that floor and the doors open.

Time Machine Meditation

Another image that I discovered lends itself very well to past-life meditation is a time machine. I prefer to visualize the one from the movie of the H. G. Wells novel by that name, but a time machine from any of your favorite time-travel movies or television shows—such as the time-traveling phone booth from the British television series "Dr. Who"—will suffice. One appealing feature of a time machine is the clock it often has on its control panel, the hands of which spin rapidly backwards as the device hurtles back through time. When visualized, this image is an especially powerful psychological cue for instructing your unconscious mind that you wish to go back to one of your previous existences.

To use a time machine as an induction image, after you are in a state of deep meditation, get into the machine, and tell it to take you to one of your previous lives. Concentrate especially on the clock moving backwards as the machine takes you back through the mists of time. After it has landed, or after you have willed it to land, simply wait for the mists to clear and proceed as with the other meditations above.

Creating Your Own Induction Image

Whether you are meditating alone or being talked through a guided meditation, one of the most important keys to success is that you feel *absolutely* comfortable about the induction image being employed. If you have claustrophobia, it is probably not a good idea to use a tunnel or other enclosed image. Another potential problem facing the would-be past-life explorer is that some induction images may have undiscovered and unpleasant past-life associations. For example, New York past-life therapist Roger Woolger frequently uses the image of a bridge when guiding his patients through past-life meditations. However, he told me that he has occasionally run into problems when patients suddenly remember being killed on bridges in former lifetimes. His wife, Jennifer Woolger, also a past-life therapist, says that she has encountered similar difficulties when using the image of a boat and even an elevator, and both agree that no single image is foolproof.[4]

Thus, before you embark on a past-life meditation, you may try to sense any past-life resonance for a particular image, or consult your unconscious mind with a pendulum to see if the image you have chosen is right for you. If you are not comfortable with any of the images suggested in this chapter, you should make up your own image—a boat traveling to a magical island, a pillared colonnade in the middle of a flower-filled meadow, or even a cosmic television set whose different channels each contain one of your past lives. Similarly, you might ask your unconscious mind to give you an image that is right for you during one of your meditations, or in a dream.

Mirror Meditation

There is a variation on the solo technique that I discovered quite by accident and which can be astonishingly effective—performing a past-life meditation in front of a mirror. I have since discovered that various other researchers have also employed this technique.

To perform a mirror meditation, situate yourself in front of a large mirror and then go to Steps 1 through 6 of the basic past-life meditation. You will also need some light to perform the meditation; dim light works best, such as the light provided by a candle. When you have completed the basic meditation, instead of moving on to Step 7 and an induction image, open your eyes and meditate on your own reflection in the mirror, mentally telling yourself that soon your features will start to change and you will see yourself as you looked in one of your previous incarnations.

A word of caution: During this meditation you may see some extremely dramatic changes take place in your features. This can be quite frightening. Only perform a mirror meditation if you feel completely comfortable with this prospect. At any point during the meditation, if you become disturbed by seeing your own features change, simply end your meditation and turn a light on, and the process will stop.

What To Do If You Can't Summon Up a Past-Life Memory

If the basic meditation technique doesn't prove effective for you and changing your induction image doesn't help, there are several things you can try. First, pay close attention to the thoughts and feelings you experience while you meditate. Are you actually relaxed? Are you truly able to concentrate and keep your mind focused on the visualization image you have chosen, or do you find that a host of trivial and everyday thoughts still constantly interrupt you as you meditate? If this is the case, you simply have not yet achieved the necessary state of meditation, and you need more practice.

Trying too hard can also be a problem. Sometimes people get so nervous and filled with anticipation at the prospect of learning about their past lives that their excitement actually blocks the process. If you have reason to suspect that this may be your problem, try to take a more leisurely attitude toward your past-life explorations. During Step 6 of your meditation, after you have asked your unconscious mind to shield you against memories that are too painful for you to deal with, ask your mind to help you be patient. Tell yourself that whether you relive a past-life memory in this meditation or the next one, you are willing to wait, and that you understand that even though you are not consciously aware of it, your unconscious mind may be helping to bring about changes within your psyche that will better prepare you to relive such memories.

Remember also that the key to success lies in *not thinking* about what you are going to find waiting for you at the end of a tunnel or through a doorway. Don't try to second-guess your unconscious mind. Let it do the work.

If you follow this advice and still have no success, it may be that solo meditation just simply isn't the path for you. If this seems to be the case, experiment with other approaches. For example, an individual who does not have success meditating alone may find it easier to enter a state of past-life awareness when assisted by another person. Exercises for two or more individuals will be given in Part Two.

Once you have become adept at the art of relaxation and meditation, you also have all the basic skills necessary to learn how to use various self-hypnotic techniques to remember your past lives. That is the subject of the next chapter.

Endnotes

1. Swami Prabhavananda and Christopher Isherwood, trans. and commentary, *How to Know God: The Yoga Aphorisms of Patanjali* (New York: Mentor, 1953), p. 30.

2. Nyanaponika Thera, *The Heart of Buddhist Meditation* (New York: Samuel Weiser, 1962), p. 164.

3. Dr. Ernest Pecci, "President's Message," *The Association for Past-Life Research and Therapy Newsletter* 4, no. 3 (Summer 1984): 2.

4. Conversation with Roger and Jennifer Woolger, December 17, 1985.

5 ~

Self-Hypnosis Techniques

The word hypnosis means many different things to different people. For some it evokes the image of a watch-swinging Svengali. For others it is a term associated with patients lying on couches and being carefully guided back through their childhood memories by skilled psychoanalysts. If you ask five different people what hypnosis is, you will probably get five different answers.

After years of study even the scientific community is unable to completely explain what happens to people when they enter a hypnotic state. Although hypnosis superficially resembles the state achieved during meditation, studies have shown that the two are physiologically quite different. While meditating, one's oxygen consumption drops rapidly within the first five or ten minutes, but under hypnosis there is no noticeable change.[1] At the command of a hypnotist a subject can also be made to dream, but electroencephalograms, or EEGs, of the brain taken during this state have shown that "hypnotic dreams" are not the same as those we dream during sleep.[2] Indeed, based on the evidence of EEGs alone, it appears that the state of consciousness that hypnosis most closely resembles is the waking state. For many years this inspired skeptics to assert that there was no such thing as a *bona fide* state of hypnosis.

Now it is generally conceded that hypnosis is a valid phenomenon, and many researchers believe that what we call a hypnotic trance actually encompasses a range of altered states of consciousness.[3] Furthermore, although physiological evidence distinguishing hypnosis from other mental states has been a long time coming, recent research has begun to suggest that hypnosis has something to do with the so-called split brain—the fact that the brain divides up its activities between its left and right hemispheres.

It is now widely accepted that in most individuals one side of the brain is dominant over the other. One result of this lopsided division in brain activity is that most of us favor one side of our body over the other; we are either right-handed or left-handed. If you are right-handed it is a good indication that your left brain is dominant, and if you are left-handed you are probably right-brain dominant. In addition to left- or right-handedness, many other skills seem to align themselves with specific hemispheres of the brain. For example, the left brain is now believed to have more of an aptitude for language skills, categorizing and naming, marking time, counting, verbalizing, and analyzing; whereas the right brain has more of an aptitude for perceptual skills, intuition, imagination, dreaming, inventing, visualizing, understanding metaphors, being creative, and suspending all sense of time.

A research group led by psychiatrist Dr. John Gruzelier at London's Charing Cross Hospital Medical School has recently turned up evidence that individuals who have a left-brain dominance are more susceptible to hypnosis than those whose right brains are dominant. However, Gruzelier and his group have also found that, after such left-brain dominant individuals are hypnotized, their right hemispheres become the major seat of brain activity for the duration of their trance. Thus, Gruzelier concluded that the initial left-brain dominance is important because it assists the individual in achieving the finely honed focus of attention that is so necessary to going into trance. However, once such an individual enters a hypnotic trance, the right brain takes over because it is the side of the brain that already possesses a natural aptitude for dreamlike perceptions, visualization, and suspended time sense.[4]

The lesson to be gleaned from the complexity of the hypnosis phenomenon is that we should never underestimate the seemingly unending vistas of the human mind. Although all methods for unearthing past-life memories involve some sort of contact with the unconscious, the mental states associated with each of these methods are unique and possess their own subtleties and differences. In practice, one of the major differences between meditation and self-hypnosis is that self-hypnosis relies on some sort of lulling and monotonous visual image to induce an altered state of consciousness. This state of consciousness is very similar to the entranced feeling you get if you spend several minutes watching the median line on a highway go by, and even the sort of timeless sense you lapse into if you become overly engrossed in a television show.

Hypnosis also creates a state of heightened suggestibility. This appears to be because the right brain does not analyze things with the same rigid logic and scrutiny as the left brain. The right brain accepts what is told to it with childlike innocence. It is passive and obedient. When asked for information, it often supplies it in magnificently detailed pictures. This makes hypnosis an especially good tool for exploring past-life memories.

Basic Self-Hypnosis Technique

In this chapter we will look at several past-life remembering techniques that involve self-hypnosis. Unlike past-life meditations, the self-hypnotic techniques described in this chapter generally do not result in an immediate past-life recollection. Rather, they are designed to encourage the mind to remember past-life memories in the form of intuitive flashes throughout the day and occasionally in the form of dreams during sleep. They are also very safe and gradual methods for recalling past lives as they allow the inner self to retain control of both the subject matter and the timing of the appearance of these memories.

I have not included any information about how to hypnotize another individual, because I feel that is a process best done by a trained professional. There will be more on this subject in the chapter on finding a past-life therapist.

What follows is the basic technique for self-hypnosis for past-life recollection.

Step 1—Choose a place to perform the technique As with meditation, you should perform self-hypnosis in a room where you feel completely comfortable and will not be interrupted. It is easier to enter a state of light trance if the room is fairly warm. Until you become proficient in entering a light trance, you should choose an object on which to fix your attention. It may be a spot on the ceiling or wall, a fire in a fireplace, an image turning around and around on a phonograph record, a sparkling crystal pendant, or even just a burning candle.

Step 2—Focus your attention on the object and relax After making yourself comfortable, fix your attention on the object (for the sake of this exercise we'll use a candle), and start to regulate your breathing until your exhalations are deep, long, and relaxed. Try to shut out all other thoughts as you focus on nothing but the flickering candle, its warmth and brightness, and the glowing nimbus of light surrounding it. Tell yourself: "As I watch this candle flame I'm going to become more and more relaxed. All tension is draining out of my body, and my eyelids are becoming heavy. Soon they will be so heavy that I will no longer be able to keep them open."

Step 3—Close your eyes and imagine that all tension is leaving your body After a minute or two of meditating on the candle flame, and after you start to be lulled by the flickering flame, say, "Now I am going to sink into a deep state of relaxation." Then close your eyes and move your concentration slowly through your body, making sure everything is relaxed. Feel your toes become relaxed. Feel all tension seep out of your legs, arms, neck, and shoulders. Let your back and facial muscles relax.

Step 4—Visualize yourself descending a set of stairs As soon as you feel very calm and relaxed, tell yourself, "Now I am going to go deeper into a state of hypnosis." When you say this, visualize yourself walking down a circular staircase and continue to say "deeper, deeper," as you descend the stairs. After you have moved partway down the stairs, imagine that you only have ten more steps to go. Visualize your feet as they continue to go down . . . down . . . and count backwards from ten, giving each step a number. Imagine that you reach the foot of the steps when you reach "one" and that when you look before you, there is a comfortable room and a bed awaiting you. You walk over to the bed, and the moment you lie down on it, you feel a pleasant, sinking feeling as if you are whisked off into an even more deep and relaxed state. As you continue to lie in the bed, you feel more relaxed and more enclosed by a protective and peaceful darkness than you have ever felt.

Step 5—Tell yourself that soon you will remember something about one of your past lives Once you are comfortably ensconced in this darkness, tell yourself either aloud or mentally, "Now, I am in a deep state of hypnosis. When I awaken, I will be fully relaxed and refreshed. Sometime during the next several weeks I am going to remember something about one of my past lives. I will recall a memory that I will feel very comfortable with and which will teach me something that it is important for me to know in this life." After giving yourself this suggestion, repeat it once or twice, slowly and gently, just to make sure your unconscious mind has received the message. Then, just continue to relax for a while. When you are ready to come out of your light trance, tell yourself, "Now I am going to wake up. I am going to count to ten, and when I reach ten, I will be fully refreshed and awake." Then count yourself back out.

Remember to perform this procedure slowly, giving yourself at least ten or twenty minutes to go through the steps. Although you may get results following the first session, the more you practice, the deeper the trance state you will enter. The purpose of entering a light trance is to make your unconscious mind much more receptive to the suggestions you give it. Thus, you can also use this technique to reprogram yourself in any desired area, such as telling yourself your study habits will improve, your depressions will weaken and go away, your health will improve, your desire for cigarettes will lessen, and so on.

If you use this technique for past-life exploration, it is important to practice it on a regular basis for at least a couple of weeks. As promised, the past-life information, when it comes, will present itself in the form of intuitive flashes. You must be ready to focus on them and remember them when they occur, so your memories do not slip back into your unconscious like forgotten dreams. For example, once while taking an early morning stroll down Central Park West in New York, I found myself thinking, "God, the color the sunlight makes on these buildings really reminds me of St. Petersburg." The thought was so fleeting and seemed so self-evident at the time that I nearly didn't stop and take conscious note of either its unusual nature or the fact that I have never been in St. Petersburg in this lifetime. Be on guard for such sudden realizations. If, on focusing on such a thought, you realize that you have no conscious intellectual reason for making a given association, repeat the thought several times in your mind, or make a note of it, so that you do not forget it. Then write it down in your journal as a piece of possible past-life information.

Self-Hypnosis Through Repeated Suggestion

If you find that visualization is not your forte and that you are a much more verbal or right-brain-dominant individual, an alternative method is simply to repeat your request over and over again for a period of time. To take this route, follow the procedure for self-hypnosis through repeated suggestion.

Follow Steps 1 through 3 of the basic self-hypnosis technique for remembering past lives. Then, once you have reached the point where you are completely relaxed and all tension has left your body, recite the following suggestion either mentally or aloud: "Sometime over the course of the next week I am going to remember one of my past lives." Keep repeating the same words over and over again for a period of five minutes making sure that no other thoughts or images intrude while you do this. Try to sense the meaning of the statement as you repeat it, and do not simply allow it to become a stream of meaningless syllables that you recite by rote.

After you have done this for five minutes, relax for a few moments more. When you are ready, tell yourself, "Now I am going to wake up. I am going to count to ten, and when I reach ten, I will be fully refreshed and awake." Then count yourself back out.

Because this method leaves the choice of which past-life memory you will remember entirely up to your unconscious mind, you do not have to worry about painful memories surfacing too quickly. You can also substitute other requests in this exercise. For example, they might include a more general request such as, "I am going to start remembering my past lives," or something as specific as "I am going to remember more about the lifetime I had in Vienna." You could even ask directly for help in other past-life recall techniques: "The next time I meditate I am going to enter the deepest and most relaxed trance that I have ever been in."

Remember that, if you do substitute a specific request, you should make sure to word it in a way that will prevent painful past-life information from surfacing too quickly. For instance, you might say, "When I am ready, I am going to remember more about the lifetime I had in Vienna." Or, "I am going to remember more helpful and happy memories from the lifetime I had in Vienna."

Remember also that the more you practice this exercise, the more dramatic the results. Although once a day is ideal, three or four times a week will suffice until you achieve your desired goal.

The Index Card Technique

Another extremely safe method for recalling past lives and a very successful approach for many people (including skeptics) is simply to write your request on an index card and glance at the card at least ten or fifteen times a day for several weeks. The request can be worded according to the suggestions above. The only difference between this and the other techniques is that instead of communicating the message to your unconscious mind while in a trance state, you communicate it to your unconscious mind in the same way that you communicate to it any habit or automatic ability, through repetition. As directed in the chapter on dreams, make up several index cards and place them where you will see them often during the course of your day—on your bathroom mirror, on your nightstand, in a desk drawer that you open frequently, and so on. Each time you spot the card, run the message silently through your thoughts. If you have the mental discipline to do this without resorting to such memory aids, you can forego writing the message down and simply repeat it silently whenever you think of it. However, it is very important that you do this at least ten times a day to make sure that the message is actually getting through to your unconscious mind.

As with the basic self-hypnotic technique, by following this procedure for a couple of weeks—or even by adopting it as a regular habit—you will find that your unconscious mind will eventually answer your request by tossing up amazing pieces of information for your conscious perusal. These will take the form of intuitive flashes, so you needn't become concerned that you are going to lose consciousness or drift off into trance at inopportune moments during the day. For example, just as you are about to take a sip of coffee, in the flash of a second, you may suddenly become aware of how fond you were of drinking tea in ancient China. What is interesting about brief remembrances called forth by using this method is that sometimes you will find yourself fondly pondering a past-life event for several seconds before it even occurs to you that the scene is no longer part of your daily life. I have had this happen to me on numerous occasions, and it is a striking experience.

Like the Resonance Method, self-hypnotic techniques for past-life exploration are an excellent adjunct to other methods and can be particularly useful in determining different time periods and cultures on which you should concentrate further efforts. However, self-hypnotic techniques are also excellent "warm up" exercises for preparing your unconscious mind for past-life exploration in general. Performed on a regular basis, they can actually ready your unconscious for deeper exploration and enhance your chances of success with other methods such as meditation and dream work.

Endnotes

1. Robert Keith Wallace and Herbert Benson, "The Physiology of Meditation," in *The Nature of Human Consciousness*, ed. Robert E. Ornstein (New York: Viking Press, 1974), p. 266.

2. Ernest R. Hilgard, *The Experience of Hypnosis* (New York: Harcourt, Brace & World, 1968), p. 150.

3. Charles T. Tart, *Altered States of Consciousness* (New York: John Wiley & Sons, 1969), p. 229.

4. Liz Grist, "Hypnosis Relies on Left-Brain Dominance," *New Scientist* 103, no. 1415 (August 2, 1984): 36.

Part Two:

Exploring for Two

6 ~

Guided Meditations

The basic premise behind a guided meditation is very similar to that of individual past-life meditations, except that instead of meditating by yourself, you have someone else to talk you through all of the steps of the exercise. The benefit of this approach is that often it is easier for many of us to take slow, deep breaths, to relax different parts of our bodies, and to keep our thoughts focused on a particular visualization when we have someone else guiding us through the process. One risk in the approach is that you are no longer the sole overseer of which past-life events are unearthed. Your guide or facilitator must therefore be careful not to steer you into a past-life memory that is too painful for you to deal with.

Basic Technique for Guided Past-Life Meditation

The first thing that you should do if you decide to experiment with guided meditation is to choose a partner with whom you feel totally at ease. I recommend that you perform your guided meditation in private or in the presence of only a few close and trusted friends. There are two reasons for this. First, past-life explorations always bring with them the possibility of unearthing some very personal and intimate information, and the meditator may not feel comfortable with this surfacing in front of casual acquaintances. Second, this is not a parlor game. An atmosphere of seriousness and trust are essential for successful results.

The following instructions are for the person guiding the meditation.

Step 1—Choose a place to meditate Choose a place to meditate according to the guidelines discussed in the first chapter.

Step 2—Preliminary discussion Discuss with the meditator what he wants to accomplish. Ask him which guardian figure he would like to employ and ask him for any other messages he has for his own unconscious mind—images he wants explored, questions he wants answered.

Step 3—Tell the meditator to start to relax In a calm and gentle voice tell the meditator to close his eyes and empty his mind of all extraneous thoughts. Then assist him in relaxing by reciting the following: "Breathe in and out in long, slow, steady breaths. As you do this, focus on keeping your breathing as deep, unstrained, and relaxed as possible. Feel each breath moving slowly . . . in and out . . . in and out . . . like the gentle, peaceful waves of an evening tide. Feel all of your worries leaving you through your breath. Think of nothing but my voice as you sink slowly into a state of deep relaxation. At the count of ten you will find yourself filled with a feeling of great peace, and your unconscious mind will be able to hear everything that I have to say. One . . . Two . . . Three . . . all troublesome thoughts are now leaving your mind. Four . . . Five . . . Six . . . you can hear nothing but the sound of my voice . . . Seven . . . Eight . . . Nine . . . Ten."

Step 4—Tell the meditator what is to be accomplished Tell the meditator the goals that the two of you have discussed previously. For example: "As we continue, you are going to tell me about one of your previous lives. You will not remember any memories that are too painful for you to deal with and you will only recall incidents that will help you grow or understand something about yourself in this life. No matter how deeply you go into your own unconscious mind, you will always be safe, and you will always be able to hear my voice."

Step 5—Ask the meditator to call upon his guardian figure Continue: "We are now going to take a moment to call upon your higher self [*or other preferred guardian figure*] for protection. Mentally send a message of peace to your higher self and ask that it watch over you and help guide you to a memory that it is important for you to know. Feel the presence and the love of your higher self even now. See that love surrounding you in a beautiful cloud of radiant white light. Know that nothing harmful can get through the light. You will experience nothing painful or frightening, for your higher self is now watching over you and protecting you."

Step 6—Guide the meditator into a deeper state of meditation Say, "You are now ready to go into an even deeper state of relaxation. Your entire body is becoming weighltless . . . almost nonexistent . . . as every last trace of muscle tension evaporates. Your toes and feet are growing lighter as you search through your body and see that all muscle tension leaves. Your calves are growing lighter and more relaxed, so are your legs. Your arms feel almost as if they are floating as you drift deeper and deeper into a state of peace and relaxation. Your body is now so relaxed that it no longer feels like it is made of matter. It is made of a lighter substance, a gentle, glowing cloud of light, and you feel yourself floating . . . floating . . . in a golden sea of light. At the count of ten you will be in a state of complete relaxation. One . . . Two . . . your physical body is now completely gone, and you are a being composed of light . . .

Three . . . Four . . . you can travel anywhere you want in your body of light, and you are moving deeper and deeper into your thoughts. Nothing is holding you back, and all you can hear is the sound of my voice. Five . . . Six . . . Seven . . . you are completely weightless . . . Eight . . . Nine . . . Ten. You are now in a state of deep and total relaxation."

Step 7—Guide the meditator through a visualization Continue, "Now that you have reached this state, look before you and you will see a hallway [*or other predetermined image*]. Go into the hallway and start to walk down it. Notice the floor, how beautiful it is. There are many doorways lining the hallway, but there is one special door waiting for you at the end. As you continue to walk, you will see that it is coming into sight. It is a very beautiful door, and as you approach, it is starting to open. You are going to walk through the door and into one of your past lives. At the count of five you will walk through the door. One . . . Two . . . the door is getting closer. Three . . . it is now completely open and you are walking through it. Four . . . Five . . . you have now walked through the door, and you are in one of your past lives."

Step 8—Ask the subject to describe what he is seeing Once the subject is through the door, the first thing you should do is ask him to look down at his feet and tell you what sort of footwear he is wearing, if any. Then ask the subject to describe other features of his clothing. The most important thing to remember after guiding a subject into a state of past-life awareness is not to offer him information or conclusions about what he is seeing. For example, if he tells you that he is wearing a long robe, it does not mean that in the past life he's remembering he was a woman. He may be wearing a toga or some other similar garment. *Don't give any opinions whatsoever about the experience;* simply question the subject. What is his name? Does he know what time period he is in? (If he doesn't know, don't pressure him—many researchers have discovered that in times past a lot of people went about their daily lives without having any idea what year it was. You will have to decipher this fact from the other details the subject tells you about his surroundings. What is his gender? Career? What is he thinking about? Are there any other people present where he is? If so, who are they? What are they doing, and are the people important to him? What else does he see, and how does he feel about what he is seeing? What is important for him to know about this life? Does he know any of the people from this life in his current life? And so on.

If the meditator does happen to blunder into a painful situation, simply tell him to move ahead to another time (in that life or in another life) in which he was happy. Unless you are a trained therapist, *never* try to guide a meditator through a painful or traumatic past-life event.

Step 9—Bring the meditator back out Once you have completed the past-life exploration, tell the meditator that at the end of ten he will return to his physical body and be completely awake and refreshed. You should also tell him that he will remember everything he has experienced. Then count the subject back out. "One . . . Two . . . all feeling is returning to your body. Three . . . Four . . . Five . . . you will remember everything that you have seen and experienced. Six . . . Seven . . . you are returning back to the present. Eight . . . Nine . . . Ten. You are completely awake and totally refreshed."

If, as the meditator, you do not meet with any success conjuring up the images of one of your previous incarnations with this technique, don't give up. Try again, changing the image of the hallway in this exercise to any of the other induction images mentioned in Chapter 4 on meditation. Make sure that you do not start out with an attitude of worry over whether or not anything will happen. If you find this is the case, simply push your worry aside and have faith that you *will* remember.

Similarly, once the images do start passing though your thoughts, do not hamper their natural flow by wondering things like, "Can this be possible?" Or, "Am I making all of this up?'' This is an error I made in several of my early guided meditations, and it immediately stopped the process in its tracks. It wasn't until I learned to simply sit back and witness what my unconscious mind wanted to show me that I started having fully successful recall sessions.

The Christos Technique: Guided Meditation With Massage

The basic guided meditation given above is not the only technique that you and your partner can use to explore your previous incarnations. Another popular method for two people is known as the ''Christos Technique.'' The origin of the Christos Technique is something of a mystery. In his book *Windows of the Mind*, writer Gerry Glaskin—one of the better-known popularizers of the method—says that he first stumbled across the technique in an obscure Australian magazine.[1] In an article on the subject in *New Times*, Craig R. Waters attributes the technique to a Massachusetts couple named Diane and William Swygard.[2] Whatever its origins, the Christos Technique has become an established part of the past-life-recall repertoire, and variations of it can now be found in numerous sources. The version of the Christos Technique that I present here was taught to me by Carol Dryer.

One note before beginning! Some variations of the Christos Techinque suggest two facilitators be used so that one can massage the mediator's head while the other massages the mediator's feet. However, I have performed the Christos Technique successfully with only one facilitator, and that is the version I describe below.

Step 1—Choose a place to meditate The person who is to undergo the technique should lie down on a flat, comfortable surface. If you decide to use the floor, make sure that the meditator's head (and any other portions of his body which he deems necessary) is comfortably supported by a pillow.

The place that you use should also be quiet and dimly lit to facilitate visualization.

Step 2—Apply some mentholated ointment to the meditator's forehead and ankles Apply some mentholated ointment, such as Tiger Balm, to the "third eye" region of the meditator's forehead (just above the midpoint of the eyebrows) and to both sides of his ankles just below his anklebone. Since some mentholated ointments are more powerful than others, you may want to test the ointment on the meditator prior to performing the technique, just to make sure that it is not too strong and doesn't produce discomfort. Then you should tell the meditator to close his eyes and relax.

Step 3—Vigorously massage the places where you have applied the ointment After you have applied the ointment, with the palm of your hand vigorously massage the mediatator's third-eye regions for a minute or two. Then, using both your hands, vigorously massage first one ankle and then the other (if you have a third person assisting you, you can have him massage the meditator's ankles while you do the third-eye region). Once you have massaged the subject's ankles for a minute or two, return to his third eye, and repeat the process once again. Use just enough force so that the meditator's body jiggles while you do this, but not so much force that it is an unpleasant sensation for him. (Note: One of the purposes of this vigorous massage is to help place the meditator in an even deeper state of relaxation.)

Step 4—After the meditator is relaxed, talk him through a series of visualizations When you have massaged the meditator for four or five minutes, stop and sit back quietly. Then say: "Now I want you to imagine that you are growing several inches longer than the bottom of your feet. Spend as long as you need to do this, and once you feel that you are actually extending several inches beyond the feet, let me know."

As soon as the meditator informs you that he can feel

himself extending out into space beyond his feet, tell him to shrink back to normal size.

Tell him: "Now I want you to do the same thing with your head. Feel yourself grow several inches beyond the top of your skull. Focus all of your powers of imagination on this, and as soon as you feel that you can actually sense yourself extending into the space above the top of your head, let me know."

Again, as soon as the meditator has accomplished this, tell him to shrink back to normal size. Repeat this process, only this time tell him to feel himself extending several *feet* below the bottom of his feet, then, several feet above the top of his head. Make sure that you do not rush him. Stress to the meditator that he can take as long as he feels is necessary to truly feel the sensation of having expanded beyond his normal size.

In the final stage of this process tell him: "Now I want you to sense that your entire body is blowing up like a balloon. Not only are you extending several feet beyond the soles of your feet and the top of your head, but every portion of your body is now extending several feet beyond your physical form. Actually try to sense the air around you. Feel what it's like to extend through the floorboards [*or the springs of the mattress*] beneath you. Sense yourself as a huge, weightless, air-filled giant, and tell me when you feel that you have accomplished this task."

As soon as the meditator tells you that he can feel his entire body extending out in space, have him shrink quickly back to normal size. Then repeat the balloon visualization, only this time ask him to grow even larger than before. In the third round of this stage of the exercise, instead of telling the meditator to blow up like a balloon, tell him: "Now you feel yourself leaving your body altogether. Feel yourself soaring up through space. Now I want you to see yourself settling down gently on the roof of your house [*or apartment building*]. Once you feel yourself there, tell me whether it is day or night."

If the meditator says that it is night, tell him to turn the night into the daytime. Conversely, if he says that it is daytime, tell him to turn the daytime into night. Repeat this stage of the exercise, first having the meditator describe the climate he is experiencing and then asking him to change it to some other type of climate. For example, have him change a sunny day into a snowy one, or a clear night into a rainy and fog-filled morning. (Note: It is very important that during this exercise the meditator feels that he is in complete control of the environment he is experiencing.)

Step 5—Have the meditator fly high above the earth and then come down in one of his past lives Once the meditator can effortlessly control his visualized environment, say: "Now I want you to fly up and away from the rooftop you are standing on. Keep on flying through the clouds and the upper atmosphere until you are high above the Earth. When you feel yourself suspended out in space, look back at the Earth, and see it spinning slowly beneath you. Imagine that with each spin it is going farther and farther back in time. Keep watching it spin until you feel an impulse to return. Then stop the spinning globe by setting your foot down firmly on its surface. Once you have done this, look down and see which continent you have placed your foot on."

You are now ready to proceed with all the questions listed in the basic, guided past-life meditation. It is always most important that the meditator go with the flow of what he is seeing. For example, one of the first times I underwent the Christos Technique, I succeeded quite nicely in seeing where my foot had landed on the Earth, what sort of footwear and clothing I was wearing, and even my surroundings. But then, in spite of the fact that all these images had come to me effortlessly and without any prior intellectual fantasizing, I started worrying, and the process went awry. It wasn't until I was able to "go with the flow," so to speak, that I was able to continue.

If you have a similar problem, simply remember that the ultimate source of the information you are receiving doesn't matter. Perhaps it is a past-life memory, or perhaps it is just a series of symbolic images bubbling up from your unconscious. What *is* important is that when performed properly, the Christos Technique can produce extremely startling results. The images you witness are valid messages from your own unconscious mind. Learn from them and use them to probe deeper into your own inner self.

Endnotes

1. Gerry Glaskin, *Windows of the Mind* (New York: Delacorte Press, 1974), p. 1.

2. Craig R. Waters, "You Are There," *New Times*, February 20, 1978, p. 56.

7 ~

The Active Imagination Technique

Another method for past-life recollection that lends itself to use by two people is the active-imagination technique. This was first mentioned in the chapter on dreams (see pp. 67–9). As you have read, active imagination is a technique where you enter a state of relaxation and simply allow your imagination to take a dream image and run free with it. As with meditation, if you find that you have difficulty doing this, it may be easier to have someone talk you through a series of images rather than try to conjure them up completely on your own.

Step 1—Find a comfortable place to conduct the exercise and have the imaginer enter a state of relaxation For relaxation techniques, review Steps 2 through 4 in Dream Technique Number 1 (see pp. 58–9).

Step 2—Ask the imaginer to visualize the dream image that he wishes to explore further Once the imaginer has quieted his thoughts and feels relaxed, have him visualize the dream image that he wishes to explore. You should, of course, have him choose a dream image that he suspects has some sort of past-life connotation. As an alternative, he may also choose an image that came to him during a meditation or some other past-life exploration technique.

Step 3—Tell the subject to hold the image in his mind until it starts to change and a scene unfolds When the subject has chosen an image, have him spend a few moments simply holding the image in his mind until it starts to change and become active. Once the image has become active, your primary role is to listen and help the imaginer to allow the image to develop according to its own internal directives, with as little interference or coloring on your part as possible.

What follows is a sample conversation based on an actual active-imagining session. Since each active-imagining session will develop in its own unique way, this doesn't represent what necessarily will happen if you use this technique. It should, however, give you some idea of how to proceed. The imaginer in this session has had a recurring dream of a tropical beach that he feels has some past-life meaning. The active-imagining session thus begins with the imaginer holding the beach scene in his mind.

IMAGINER: It's starting to change.

YOU: What do you see?

IMAGINER: I see palm trees and the wind is blowing. It seems like some sort of storm is going on.

YOU: Do you see anything else?

IMAGINER: I see a young couple. They're standing together on some high place and they're watching the storm. They seem to be lovers, but they also seem to be troubled by something. The image is changing very quickly now. I see lots of images, long boats, flashes of scenes depicting what it must have been like to live on the island.

YOU: Is the young couple involved in any of this activity?

IMAGINER: I'm not sure. I don't really see the faces of any of the people in the boats. It doesn't seem that important. Now I see the young couple again. They're still watching the storm.

YOU: How do you feel emotionally about the young couple?

IMAGINER: I'm worried for them. I like them.

YOU: Which one do you identify with more?

IMAGINER: I feel more for the woman. But I feel like I'm the man.

YOU: Pretend that right this moment you are the man. What do you feel or see?

IMAGINER: This is funny, but I feel that it's wrong that people think we should be ashamed.

YOU: Ashamed over what?

IMAGINER: I don't know, but suddenly I see the image of a village. There's one hut in particular, and in the hut there's an old woman. I'm not sure quite how, but somehow the the old woman has something to do with the shame. I don't know if it's something we did or something she did, but she's a part of my family, and somehow disgrace has come down on all of us for some reason.

YOU: Why don't you try pretending that you are the old woman? What does she feel and what does she see?

IMAGINER: She sees people looking at her and she knows that they are thinking about her disgrace. This bothers her, but she doesn't show it. She's very stalwart, like steel. She also knows that we don't really care about the shame and that

> leaves her with a funny feeling. A part of her thinks that it's right that we don't care, but another part of her is resentful that she sort of has to carry the burden all by herself. Oh, I think the shame has something to do with our relationship. I don't see anything really, but I get the sense that maybe I was married, or promised to someone else or something. We've broken the rules by falling in love, and it's considered very wrong, a very big deal. Now I'm the guy looking at the storm again. We're wondering just a little whether the wrong we have committed has caused this storm to come. But mostly we almost feel kind of glad. It's like we know the storm is going to cause a lot of damage to the village, but we don't care. We think that the village deserves it.

On realizing that the theme of this apparent past-life memory was not caring about shame, the imaginer became aware that in his current life he also was embroiled in a situation which had the potential of becoming a family disgrace. Indeed, this seems to be why the "storm is brewing" scene surfaced in his active-imagining session. He examined his feelings on the matter and discovered that in truth he did not feel that the situation was disgraceful at all, but was mainly worried about the feelings of his family. He also realized that he believed his family was wrong to feel any shame about the situation and (once again) was mainly feeling guilty because he did not feel any shame.

Understanding all of this (and perceiving that his unconscious mind was warning him to take another look at the matter before another metaphorical storm hit), he decided to stop feeling guilty and reconcile his feelings with his convictions.

It should be noted that because of its extremely free and wide-ranging nature, the active-imagination technique is capable of producing a vast array of information, and not all of it is as specific or useful as the example given here. As a consequence be cautious and discerning about the information you uncover in this manner. Don't necessarily assume that a sequence of images should be interpreted literally, and don't jump to conclusions. Instead, use the active-imagination technique as a method for obtaining possible clues rather than cold, hard facts about your past lives. Occasionally you will get a remarkably coherent story out of it, but just as frequently you will get a lot of chaff with your wheat.

Be prepared, also, to put in some practice hours before you and you partner really get the technique perfected. Sometimes it takes a while for your unconscious mind to fully understand what you want out of it. When it does, you will find that the active-imagination technique can be most useful for quickly conjuring up a flow of ore from the deeper levels of your psyche.

Part Three:

Exploring with Professional Guidance

8 ~

Exploring with a Professional Past-Life Therapist

If after trying the methods given in this book, you decide that you would like to make even deeper and more extensive explorations of your past-life memories, the best thing for you to do is to seek the assistance of a trained past-life professional. Past-life therapy is not for people who have a single symptom they want explained or who only want to find out one thing about the past but are unwilling to look at their entire life (or lives) as an interconnected and ongoing process. As psychologist Ronald Wong Jue observes, "Life is not a series of symptoms and symptoms relieved. Peoples' lives are usually a matrix of involvements."[1]

Most past-life professionals agree and point out that past-life therapy is only for people who have a powerful urge to grow and stretch beyond the boundaries of their present psychological, emotional, and spiritual selves, and also have the courage to look at themselves honestly and recognize that such changes may involve many levels of awareness, behavior, and patterns of social and personal interaction. Above all, a willingness for honest self-understanding is essential. As Dr. Hazel Denning warns, "You can fool yourself, even in past-life therapy. If you're not ready to look at something, you won't. Past-life therapy is not for everyone. Past-life therapy does not work for people who have not the strength to look at their own weaknesses and past transgressions, and many people cannot handle the truth about themselves. It boils down to this: Reincarnation and past-life therapy teach you to be absolutely responsible for yourself. If you can't do that, you're not going to look at something that shows you that you chose the experience, subconsciously of course. So, if you have lousy parents, it's very difficult to say, I chose them, I chose them for a reason. It's my fault they treated me that way. That's not easy."[2]

However, for those who do have the courage to explore the inner regions of their psyche and face whatever they find there, the rewards of working with a past-life therapist are great.

How to Find a Professional Past-Life Therapist

One of the best ways to find a good past-life therapist is to have one recommended by a friend whose judgment you know and trust. If you are not fortunate enough to have friends who can help you in this manner, an alternative is to contact the Association for Past-Life Research and Therapy. The association maintains a directory of past-life therapists, including their qualifications and years of practice, and lists them according to geographic area. Although most of their listings are for therapists in the United States, they do have some international listings. The directory is available to nonprofessionals who, by paying a small membership fee, have become either associate or student members of the association. For further information, write The Association for Past-Life Research and Therapy, P.O, Box 20151, Riverside, CA 92516. If you have a holistic doctor or live in a community large enough to have encouraged the formation of a New Age organization, you can also try contacting them and asking if they know of any past-life therapists whom they might recommend.

Once you have one or more names to choose from, consider the experience and credentials of each therapist. Virtually ever therapist I have talked to during the course of my research has agreed that, in addition to having experience in past-life work, it is absolutely essential that a past-life therapist have training in other psychotherapeutic and counseling techniques as well. Only a trained professional will know how to release and properly handle the powerful emotions that may surface during a past-life regression.

The second most commonly offered piece of advice when seeking a past-life therapist is to follow your instincts. For example, Hazel Denning, Executive Director of the Association for Past-Life Research and Therapy, tells all callers seeking referrals to telephone a prospective past-life therapist and see how they feel about the therapist after talking to them for a few minutes. As she explained, it is important for an individual to feel comfortable and at ease with a therapist in order for any regression technique to work. Other past-life professionals agree. If you do not like or trust a past-life therapist after talking to or meeting with him, this is a powerful indication that he is not the right therapist for you. You should apologize for taking up his time and continue your search.

In a recent article on the subject Dr. Ernest Pecci offers several useful pointers for evaluating past-life therapists:

1. Only go to a past-life therapist who charges hourly rates that are in the same range as those charged by conventional psychotherapists in your area and be wary of past-life therapists who charge excessive hourly rates, regardless of their justifications for their prices (such as the participation of spirit guides or teachers).

2. Avoid past-life therapists who focus on alleviating isolated symptoms by conjuring up a past-life event for each (like treating all pains with aspirin), without regard for the mind, body, and psyche of an individual as a whole, and without regard for the importance of integrating past-life experiences into one's current life.
3. Similarly, be wary of past-life therapists who maximize the importance of past-life events and assert that they are the cause of all present symptoms and problems.[3]

In addition to being useful criteria for evaluating potential therapists, these last two pieces of advice can also be extremely helpful in deciding whether you are ready for past-life therapy. It bears repeating that past-life therapy should not be viewed as something to do merely for recreation or in the same context as a visit to a fortune-teller. It is a powerful and transformative tool and few who undergo it come out unchanged.

Therapeutic Approaches Now Available

Once you have made the decision to go to a past-life therapist, you will have to decide what type of regression technique might be best for you. What follows is a brief summary of some of the therapeutic approaches now available.

Hypnosis

Of all methods for tapping into past-life memories, many believe that hypnosis is the most expeditious. In a hypnotic trance not only do memories have a tendency to come to the fore more rapidly than with many other methods of recall, but often quite a number of the subject's past lives become instantly accessible.

Although there is little doubt that hypnosis is one of the most powerful and extraordinary tools currently available for exploring past lives, it is also a complex and multifaceted phenomenon. Before you can make an intelligent decision as to whether a visit to a hypnotherapist is the right avenue of past-life exploration for you, there are a number of things that you should know and consider.

Hypnosis is most frequently described as a state of heightened suggestibility. This is because the merest suggestion on the part of a hypnotist often will be perceived as reality by the hypnotized subject. If a hypnotist suggests to a subject that he has no feeling in his hand, the hand of a good hypnotic subject will become numb. Similarly, if the hypnotist suggests that an onion actually smells like a rose or that there is a giant Easter rabbit standing in the room, a hypnotized individual will perceive these suggestions as equally real.

It should be pointed out immediately that the suggestibility of a hypnotized subject does not extend into areas of ethical or moral transgression. In spite of the bad press occasionally given hypnosis by horror films, numerous scientific studies have amply demonstrated that no one can be made to do anything in a hypnotic trance that they wouldn't do in their waking state. You cannot be made to kill a person, or stroll out in front of a truck, while you are hypnotized unless you have already consciously planned to do such thing. Studies have shown that even when hypnotists try to come up with elaborate and clever lies to convince a subject that he must commit a certain transgression, rather than go against his inner directives, a subject will simply come out of trance. However, tell a subject undergoing a painful dental procedure that he will need no anesthetic and feel no pain and (given that the individual trusts the hypnotist and perceives no threat) he will immediately oblige. No one really knows how the mind is able to achieve such control.

Occasionally critics of hypnotic past-life regression have challenged its validity on the grounds that hypnosis is such a highly suggestible state that asking a hypnotized individual to "Tell me about one of your past lives" cannot help but elicit a positive response. What such critics fail to take into account is that an experienced past-life hypnotherapist is well aware of this fact and will always try to avoid leading questions. For example, instead of asking a hypnotized individual "What is the past-life cause of your current back problems?" a hypnotherapist might ask simply, "What is the cause of your current back problems?" This way, if there is a past-life cause, the unconscious mind will offer it up freely without feeling obliged to fabricate an imaginary past-life event if there is no real one that is relevant.

Research has shown that roughly 90 percent of the population can be hypnotized and that like any talent, hypnotic susceptibility varies from person to person. Although only about 10 percent of the population can enter an extremely deep or somnabulistic trance, doctors who use hypnosis in place of conventional anesthesia—such as Philadelphia plastic surgeon Dr. Frank Marlowe—have found that 75 percent of the population can be hypnotized deeply enough to feel no pain during surgery.[4] It was once believed that women were more hypnotizable than men, but it is now believed that hypnotic susceptibility has nothing to do with sex, or intelligence (children, however, are more susceptible than adults). Research suggests that to some extent the ability to be hypnotized can be learned. With practice, perseverance, and the right chemistry between subject and hypnotist, many individuals who have had difficulty going under can be hypnotized at some point in their lives.

Perhaps that most distinguishing characteristic of a hypnotic past-life regression is the vividness of the experience. When hypnotically regressed by a trained professional, individuals report that they are able to hear, smell, feel, and taste various stimuli around them as vividly as if they were really there. Emotions experienced during the reliving of such past-life situations are equally immediate and real. The desirability of such vividness is a matter of personal preference. If the thought of such a vivid past-life experience excites you, or if you are skeptical and feel that seeing one of your past lives in concrete detail is the only way you will become convinced of the validity of the experience, these are factors to consider. Conversely, if after reading about hypnotism you decide that it is not right for you, you can seek instead the services of a past-life therapist who specializes in some other approach, such as guided meditation or dream work.

However, do not let the vividness of a hypnotic past-life experience by itself frighten you away from choosing past-life hypnotherapy. Remember that an experienced past-life hypnotherapist will still allow you to set your own pace and will always consult your unconscious mind and wait for its permission before embarking on any past-life exploration. Similarly, an experienced past-life therapist will also always watch out for your emotional and psychological well-being and would never allow you to languish in a painful or frightening past-life memory should one come to the surface.

If it does become necessary for you to work through a traumatic memory, there are many ways that a past-life hypnotherapist can guide you through the experience without subjecting you to undue shock or pain. For example, your hypnotherapist may give you a posthypnotic suggestion to confront the difficult memories at a later date, and only after their painful elements have been diffused.

Group Hypnotic Regression

If the idea of hypnotherapy appeals to you, another option is to be hypnotized in a group session. Such group past-life seminars have become very popular around the country, and it is quite possible that you can find one being conducted in your area. One of the advantages of such an approach is that it can be a quick and readily accessible way for you to get a "taste" of what past-life regression is all about. To some extent, attending a group session can also be a way for you to determine how susceptible you are as a hypnotic subject and enable you to decide whether past-life hypnotherapy is the right avenue for you to take. However, if you do decide to participate in a group situation, remember that it is still important to check on the credentials and experience of the individual conducting the session.

As for the disadvantages of the group approach, one is that your past-life experience by necessity cannot be as extensive or personalized as the past-life work that takes place during an individual session.

Some past-life researchers have also argued that in attending a group regression, one runs the risk of experiencing a traumatic past-life situation without the immediate therapeutic follow-up work necessary to release and heal the traumatic memory. To safeguard against this possibility, an experienced hypnotherapist will always start out by giving the group a specific hypnotic suggestion to remember only positive events. However, this is something you should inquire about before committing yourself to a group situation.

Guided Meditation

Not all past-life therapists use hypnosis. Many prefer to employ different forms of guided meditation as regression tools. The specifics of this approach have already been covered both in Chapter 4 on individual meditation and Chapter 6 on guided meditation.

Dream Work

If you are the sort of individual who has a vivid dream life or has some other reason to believe that dreams are a particularly useful way for you to communicate with your unconscious mind, you may want to look for a therapist who employs dream work in his practice.

The Netherton Method

One of the most interesting of the recently developed techniques for unearthing past-life information comes from California psychologist Morris Netherton. Netherton's method does not involve any sort of altered state of consciousness, but instead relies on repeating emotionally laden key phrases to bring about past-life recall.

The basic wisdom behind Netherton's technique—that the recurrent themes in our speech contain hidden and unconscious information about our inner selves—is not new. It is also the basis for therapeutic techniques found in Gestalt psychology, the branch of psychology that emphasizes behavior rather than introspection as the key to a person's personality. What *is* new is Netherton's discovery that recurrent themes in our speech can also be remarkably effective in unearthing our past-life memories.

In employing Netherton's technique, the past-life therapist first talks to the patient about his medical and family history and discusses the problems as the patient perceives them. During this conversation the therapist pays careful attention to any expressions or turns of phrase that the patient gives special emphasis or returns to again and again. For example, the therapist may find that the patient repeatedly refers to various situations in his life as "suffocating" or he may sum up every problem by saying, "I've tried everything and it's hopeless." After isolating a phrase, the therapist then asks the patient to lie down and concentrate on the word or words, repeating them until an additional phrase or mental picture pops into his mind. As Netherton states, "At this point most patients fear that they will draw a blank—that they will 'flop.' But almost without exception the constant repetition of a phrase will jog the patient's mind to an image, and we will work forward from there. Frequently, when a new patient finally breaks through to his first past-life image, the scene will develop at a gallop, shocking the patient and almost overwhelming him."[5]

For example, Netherton cites the case of a twenty-four-year-old office worker who sought Netherton's help because she suffered from an inexplicable and overwhelming feeling of unhappiness that she could not shake. During the course of their introductory conversation Netherton discovered that the patient returned repeatedly to three phrases, "being shoved and bumped," "unable to get my breath," and "stuck in a mess." The phrases became especially prominent when she described the "awful mess" of her office, and how she often had to leave just to be able to get her breath.

Netherton pointed out these phrases and asked the patient if they brought any images into her mind. A quizzical look crossed her face. "Well, this is my house," she replied suddenly. "I guess I'll just have to live here." Realizing that he was onto something, Netherton repeated this phrase until she described a previous existence in which she had been a black slave punished for insubordination by being locked in a small crate. As she explained, living in such close confines and being forced to breathe the fetid, repulsive air of her own filth had been unbearable for her, and at an unconscious level she was still haunted by the memory of being "shoved and pushed around" as a slave, of "being unable to breathe," and of being confined in such an "awful mess."[6]

In his book *Past Lives Therapy* (coauthored with Nancy Shiffrin), Netheron gives many instances of spontaneous regressions and healings as the result of the repetition of such emotionally laden phrases.

Regression Techniques Employing Body Massage

Some past-life therapists also employ body massage as a regression technique. The purpose and degree to which massage is used by therapists varies. For example, some therapists use massage simply as an adjunct to other regression techniques, often to assist a patient in coming to grips with a memory involving some past-life body injury.

However, there are also some therapists who use massage as their primary regression tool. One such therapist is retired California eurythmics teacher Kay Ortman. Ortman regresses people simply by massaging them for several hours while playing emotionally stirring music, such as works by Bach. Her patients who have undergone her technique assert that it is remarkably effective. As a contributing editor of *Human Behavior* stated in an article on Ortman's work: "What happened in that room during the next five hours was the strangest experience of my life. . . . I took no drugs. I was not in a trance, nor asleep and dreaming . . . [as] images of other times and places moved fleetingly through my consciousness." The editor concluded that his massage regression "had a profound influence" on the way he perceives himself and others, and that he is "no longer skeptical about reincarnation."[7]

* * *

There are many therapeutic techniques for accessing memories from previous incarnations. Some therapists employ the use of psychics, and others even use drugs to unlock past-life memories. In the end, as with most things, it all comes down to one's own personal requirements and preferences. However, the information discussed in this chapter should provide a useful basis for you to choose which technique would be the best for you if you decide that you want to be regressed by a professional.

Endnotes

1. Ronald Wong Jue, Ph.D., "Past Life Therapy: Assumptions, Stages and Process," *The Association for Past-Life Research and Therapy Newsletter* 4, no. 2 (Spring 1984): 6.

2. Conversation with Dr. Hazel Denning, January 22, 1986.

3. Dr. Ernest F. Pecci, "President's Message." *The Association for Past-Life Research and Therapy Newsletter* 4, no. 2 (Spring 1984): 2.

4. Joanne Silberner, "Hypnotism Under the Knife," *Science News* 129, no. 12 (March 22, 1986): 187.

5. Morris Netherton, Ph.D., and Nancy Shiffrin, *Past Lives Therapy* (New York: Ace Books, 1978), pp. 24–25.

6. Ibid., pp. 45–46.

7. My, "Kay Ortman's Way," *Human Behavior*, May 1979, pp. 28–34.

9 ~

Exploring with Psychics and Other Metaphysical Sources

One of the most controversial yet promising avenues of past-life exploration is consultation with a psychic. For anyone who has studied the matter with a discerning and open mind there is no doubt that there exist among us talented individuals who can psychically tune in to information that they have no normal sensory means of knowing. There is also little doubt that some of these individuals can tune in to what we've been calling past-life information in this book. As for how wide-ranging is the ability of any given psychic, or how accurate is the past-life information they report, the answers to these questions are as varied as the human personality.

I have been to many psychics, and my experiences in this

regard cover the entire range of possibilities. I have considered some readings to have been complete rubbish. I have had apparently talented psychics tell me about past lives for which I felt no resonance, and I have also had others describe in detail various past-life memories that I have had since I was a child. The bottom line is that when you set out to find a talented psychic, you must be both discerning and prudent. However, when you find a psychic who is really able to "tune in" to you—and you will know when you have found one—he or she can be of great assistance in helping you explore your past-life memories.

Finding a Psychic

The best way to find a good psychic, as with finding other professionals, is through the recommendation of a friend, or even better, through the recommendation of a past-life psychologist or other New Age professional. Another possibility is to contact one of several professional organizations for psychics that have sprouted up around the country. One such organization is the Association of Psychic Practitioners in San Jose, California. Designed as both a professional organization and a sort of Better Business Bureau for psychics, the APP was founded by psychic Mary Palermo in 1980 because, as a practicing psychic consultant for more than twenty years, she was tired of being lumped in the same category as gypsy fortune-tellers and other so-called psychics of dubious ethics.

In addition to functioning as a professional association, the APP offers a certification process to honest and sincere psychics. To qualify, a psychic practitioner must sign a statement of ethics, furnish letters of reference and "self-definition," and pass an oral evaluation conducted by a panel of volunteer psychologists, professors, and other related professionals. Further information can be obtained by writing to the Association of Psychic Practitioners, P.O. Box 6892, San Jose, California 95150.

Although most of APP's professional members are on

the West Coast, there are similar organizations in other areas of the country. In the New York area the New York Spiritualists Center, Inc., and its sister organization, the Metaphysical and Parapsychological Institute, also offer referral services (for a fee) to individuals interested in finding a qualified psychic. The address for both is 225 East 74th Street, New York, New York 10021. Many communities have parapsychological or New Age organizations listed in their yellow pages that can offer such assistance. Some communities even have listings of psychics in the yellow pages, although Palermo warns that good advertising doesn't necessarily mean a good psychic. As she states, "You can't go by advertisements. Some of these psychics have wonderful press agents."[1]

Just as with finding a past-life therapist, one of the first things to consider is how you feel about your potential psychic. This is important not only because a good rapport with a psychic is necessary for a good reading, but also because our intuitions are often the best acid test for how "right" a situation is for us. Call the psychic up and simply see how you feel about him after talking for a few minutes. Carol Dryer advises that when looking for a good psychic, you should "follow your feelings. . . . If you get up to the door and you don't feel right about it, leave."[2]

In addressing the same issue, Palermo told me that she feels one should follow roughly the same procedure. She advises would-be seekers of psychic consultations not to be afraid to ask questions. Find out how many years of experience the psychic has. Find out what he charges and precisely what he offers in return for his fee. Find out what his training is, and whether he adheres to any particular school of metaphysical thought. Palermo also suggests asking a prospective psychic practitioner if it might be possible to speak to one of his clients so as to better determine both his qualifications and his sincerity (although Palermo warns that client-counselor privacy may not always permit a psychic to give out another client's name).

In shopping around for a good psychic here are several other important points to keep in mind.

- Be wary of psychics who put an overemphasis on money. For example, if a psychic seems more concerned about what's going in your wallet than what's going on in your psyche, chances are this is telling you something about him. Similarly, avoid any psychic who tells you that for a sum of money, he can remove a curse, mend your marriage, or find you a lover.

- Be wary of psychics who try to control or manipulate your life. A good psychic will offer opinions, not commands, and seldom—if ever—tell you that there is something that you absolutely must do.

- Be wary of psychics who are overly complimentary and who rattle off streams of preposterous past-life scenarios for you, such as, "You were Julius Caesar because of your great skill as a leader and then you were Michelangelo because of your extraordinary sensitivity." Similarly, be wary of psychics whose readings are nothing but platitudes and generalities that are true of everyone, such as "You do not always use your time wisely."

- Be wary of psychics who tell you that they are 100 percent accurate, or who tell you that they are somehow cosmically special and chosen and one of only a handful of psychic practitioners on the Earth who has a direct line to psychic information. No psychic is 100 percent accurate, and any psychic who tells you that he is is either misguided or lying. Similarly, be wary of psychics who tell you that the advice they give you is somehow etched in stone. A good psychic will always admit that what he is tuning in to is a realm of potentialities and probabilities. Some of the things a good psychic tells you may be "highly probable," but a talented clairvoyant will rarely—if ever—tell you that something is immutable or absolute.

- Be wary of psychics who do not want you to tape record what they tell you. Many good psychics will give you a tape recording of your reading as a matter of course, but if they do not offer to tape your consultation, be sure to tape it yourself. Often by relistening to a reading, you will gain a clearer understanding of many of the things the psychic has told you and that you may have missed the first time around.

- Be wary of psychics who try to cloak what they do in a veil of mystery, or who refuse to answer simple questions about their procedures by alleging that they do not want to give away their dark and mystical secrets. Like any other professionals, honest and sincere psychics will be open about what they do.

How Can You Tell If a Psychic Is Really Psychic?

Once you have found a psychic whom you feel is sincere and trustworthy and you have begun your consultation with him, it will rapidly become obvious whether he is psychic or not. A talented psychic will be able to readily tell you very accurate information about yourself. Depending on the skill and area of emphasis of the psychic, it may be information about your health, your psychological makeup, your relationships, or your business circumstances. Whatever the case, he will quickly reveal—via the content of what he is saying—that he is privy to information about your life that is far more specific than any facts he might have gleaned from your appearance and whatever brief introductory information you have given him. For example, I have an internal anatomical anomaly that is not visible to the naked eye, and I have found that when assessing my health, a talented sensitive will almost always pick up on this immediately.

Occasionally you may receive a reading from a psychic that will seem to make no sense. It may mean that the psychic (for reasons that will be touched on shortly) has not been able to tune in to any accurate information about you. It may mean that the psychic has told you something that you are not yet consciously ready to hear or acknowledge. Or it may mean that the psychic is a fraud. It is up to you to determine which of these three possibilities is the correct one. You should start by trying to rule out fraud. If the psychic is an established and well-known clairvoyant, or has come highly recommended to you by several of your reasonably intelligent friends, you may tentatively rule out fraud. Conversely, if the psychic tells you that you have always been celebrities in your past lives, or offers to balance your aura by selling you several hundred dollars' worth of magic crystals, you have grounds to believe that you are being bilked. If you're still unsure, play the tape of your session to a close and trusted friend, and see what his opinion is on the matter.

If, after examining the situation, you decide that the psychic is a talented and sincere clairvoyant, but the reading still makes no sense to you, consider whether the psychic has told you something that you are not ready to hear or acknowledge. There are two ways of doing this. Play the tape recording of your reading to a close and trusted friend, and ask for an honest opinion. Frequently, our close friends are able to see things in us that we are not yet ready to confront in ourselves. Another option is to put the tape aside and play it later from time to time. Psychic Carol Dryer told me that she has had clients who were initially very skeptical of what she had to say call her months and even years later to tell her that after deciding to listen to the tape one last time everything had finally, suddenly, made sense to them. (I, too, have had this experience listening to tapes of sessions at a later date.)

However, if after exploring these options you decide that an ethical, sincere, and usually very talented clairvoyant has given you a reading that is as inscrutable to you as so many hieroglyphics, do not fret. Sometimes even the best of psychics simply miss. Indeed, I have frequently found that if I recommend a talented psychic to six of my friends, although the majority of them will come back with glowing reports, at least one individual in the group will always be disappointed in the results of the session. I do not know why this is. Perhaps the friend simply wasn't ready to listen to what the psychic had to say. Perhaps, like any talented person, the psychic simply had an off day, or perhaps the chemistry between the psychic and the individual was not right. Whatever the case, many researchers have also commented on the same phenomenon, and it is a possibility to watch out for.

Once you have found a talented psychic, some of the past-life information he will tell you will just click. You will know it is correct because it will tug at something deep within you, or it will suddenly make you understand an entire constellation of information about yourself that you never understood or connected together before. On the other hand, some past-life information may not evoke any response in you and may seem no more familiar or meaningful than a page torn randomly out of a novel from the library. If you find that this is the case, you should treat the information as you would any potential past-life memory obtained by one of the methods given in this book. Look at it and assess it with the scrutiny of a psychologist, a historian, and a lawyer. Keep in mind all of the statistical realities that have been previously discussed regarding past lives, and if it remains unfamiliar, but seems as if it might have historical validity, write it down in your past-life journal, and then wait and see if you encounter any further pieces of information that either confirm or refute the information. Remember that if reincarnation is a fact, we have all lived dozens and even hundreds of lives, and not all of them are going to strike us as immediately familiar. However, remember also that no matter how uncannily accurate a psychic seems, no psychic is right all of the time, and not everything they say should be taken as gospel. Even the most talented clairvoyant can still tune into the wrong wavelength on occasion.

Accept Your Psychic's Humanity

Having chosen a clairvoyant with whom you have a good rapport, remember two important things. First, do not let your awe of his psychic abilities cloud your perception of what sort of human being the psychic is. Just as a talent to play the piano in itself tells you nothing about the integrity or wisdom of the person playing the piano, a talent for paranormal functioning does not necessarily imply an equal gift in the areas of compassion, ethics, or spiritual wisdom. Although psychic functioning can be an outgrowth of spiritual development, it can also be due to other factors as well.

Thus, no matter how dazzled you are by a psychic's ability, weigh him in his fullness, and sense how involved he is in all of the multiplicity of other areas that makes each of us human. Do not make a psychic your guru on the basis of his psychic ability alone.

Second, when you begin working with a talented clairvoyant, do not allow his skills as a psychic to persuade you that he must therefore have some corner on cosmic truth. Psychics have differences of opinion and idiosyncrasies of thought just like the rest of us, and it is doubtful whether any two clairvoyants share a completely identical cosmic world-view. Similarly, since the information a psychic receives is always filtered through his own thoughts and internal biases, no matter how talented a sensitive is, the information he channels will always be at least slightly colored and distorted by the mere fact that it is passed through him. This is perhaps why extraordinarily talented psychics almost always speckle their usually astounding pronouncements with a few unmitigated absurdities. For example, psychic Edgar Cayce, a fundamentalist Christian when not in trance, was quite accurate in most of the past-life information he delivered, but he also had a tendency to tell a statistically preponderant number of the people who came to him for past-life readings that they had had a lifetime in which they had known and talked with Christ.

The point to be gleaned from this is that, no matter how accurate a psychic seems to be, like all of us mere mortals they are also fallible. If nine of the things a talented sensitive tells you are unnervingly accurate, but the tenth seems to be nonsense, don't lose sleep trying to hammer it into your belief system. It may just be nonsense.

Past-Life Exploration Through Astrology

According to many traditions you can find out about your past lives through astrology. For example, in his book *Autobiography of a Yogi*, Paramahansa Yogananda asserts that one's astrological birth chart is actually a portrait of all the past karma and influences one has brought into this current incarnation. As he writes, "A child is born on that day and at that hour when the celestial rays are in mathematical harmony with his individual karma."[3] Thus, by having one's birth chart interpreted by a skilled astrologer, Yogananda says that one can become aware of those karmas which will have the most powerful and formative influence on one's life, and through right conduct, prayer, and spiritual self-realization one can even ameliorate negative karmas and convert what might have manifested as a "thrust of the sword" into a mere "prick of the pin." However, Yogananda warns that such information can only be gleaned from a birth chart by astrologers of "intuitive wisdom," and adds that "these are few."[4]

Many past-life researchers have also uncovered evidence suggestive of a connection between karma and astrology. For example, California past-life regressionist Dick Sutphen, who has spent nearly twenty years studying the past-life phenomenon, cites one case in which a woman described watching a group of "masters" plan her life after being hypnotically regressed to the between-life state. She noted that in addition to taking into account all of the hundreds of other human beings it was important that she interact with during her coming incarnation, her guides also took into careful consideration the multitude of astrological factors surrounding the time and place of her birth.[5]

In one intriguing study Dr. Adrian Finkelstein, an assistant professor of psychiatry at St. Luke's Medical Center in Chicago, reports that he has even found pronounced astrological similarities between his patients' current birth charts and birth charts cast from the dates of recent past-life birthdays that they were able to recall while under hypnotic regression. Although the actual dates of birth from one lifetime to the next were not the same, Finkelstein found that many astrological influences did carry over with a greater frequency than could be explained by chance alone.[6]

Indeed, a number of the past-life therapists I have talked to feel that there is a certain validity to astrology and that a talented astrologer can indeed extract at least some past-life information from a person's horoscope. However, like Yogananda, all of the researchers I talked to who were receptive to the idea of astrology warned that it is only the rare and exceptional astrologer who is able to accurately decipher such information.

Thus, if you decide that you would like to find out past-life information by using astrology, shop around for an astrologer as you would for a psychic. When you start looking for an astrologer—through the recommendations of friends, by looking in the yellow pages, or by going to a psychic fair—remember that, as with psychics, you are entering a no-man's land replete both with skilled and sincere individuals and with untalented amateurs and cons. Be discerning, draw upon all of your intuitive skills and common sense, and try to talk to other clients of a prospective astrologer before parting with your money.

Past-Life Exploration With Trance Entities

Another source of past-life information is trance entities, personalities who claim to be human (and other) souls who inhabit nonphysical levels of reality beyond our physical dimension. These entities communicate through mediums, also known as "channels," who go into a trance and then utter or write the words of the entity. Although not available as frequently for individual consultations as physics, the words and teachings of alleged discarnate entities have become very popular in tape and book form.

It is difficult to know how seriously one should take these alleged discarnate information sources. Although it is safe to say that scientists as a whole remain extremely skeptical of the trance entities phenomenon, at least some psychologists who have studied the matter have come away convinced that something important and paranormal is occurring. For instance, parapsychologist Lawrence LeShan, who has spent hundreds of hours conversing with such entities, writes in his book *Alternate Realities*, "The feeling of *really* talking to someone you had known when they were alive was often so strong it would curl your hair."[7] While admitting that at the very least some sort of telepathic phenomenon is frequently in evidence during these conversations, LeShan concedes that he still does know what to make of trance entities. Speaking at a symposium on psychic phenomena at an annual meeting of the American Psychiatric Association, he noted that there are three possible explanations: (1) such spirits are what they claim to be, (2) they are a multiple personality split-off of the medium, or (3) they are some other phenomenon not yet offered as an explanation.[8] After intensive scrutiny and investigation, LeShan has become convinced that conscious fraud is not a viable explanation in the cases he has studied.

In a recent article entitled "Close Encounters of a Fourth Kind: Working with Non-Incarnated Entities," Berkeley psychologist Kathryn Ridall notes that after years of skepticism she has also become convinced that discarnate entities are not the product of conscious fraud.[9] Whatever they are, many of the discarnate entities that are manifesting in trance mediums today are entities of impressive wisdom and intelligence and are frequently in possession of information which could only be obtained by paranormal means. They are also, almost without exception, bursting with information about the subtle mechanics of the reincarnation process. Thus, whether they are what they say they are—entities more evolved than us who inhabit nonphysical levels of reality beyond our own—or are expressions of some presently poorly understood phenomenon of the human unconscious, they are undeniably another important manifestation of the past-life phenomenon.

The Current Abundance of Discarnate Entities

Equally intriguing is the current abundance of discarnate entities. When I first became interested in the serious study of the paranormal some seventeen years ago, I was not overly impressed with the quality of the material delivered by most trance entities. A good deal of it seemed to me so much mumbo jumbo, so I concentrated my attentions in other areas. Then, in 1981, after the publication of my book *Mysticism and the New Physics*, I started receiving letters from people noting the similarity between my views and the teachings of Seth, a trance entity channeled by writer Jane Roberts. I was aware of Roberts's work and the numerous and very popular Seth books, but had avoided them because of my long-standing aversion for trance material. Nevertheless, my curiosity was aroused, and I decided to take a look at the Seth material.

To my great surprise—and slight annoyance—I found that Seth eloquently and lucidly articulated a view of reality that I had arrived at only after great effort and an extensive study of both paranormal phenomena and quantum physics (the branch of physics that deals with subatomic particles). Moreover, he went far beyond what I had to say and offered a panoramic view of the cosmic workings of the universe that includes but greatly surpasses our current scientific (and spiritual) understandings. Of course, there is no way at present to determine whether Seth's views are correct, but they had a great intuitive impact on me and have clearly had a similar impact on the tens of thousands of other readers who anxiously awaited the publication of each new Seth book before Roberts's untimely death in 1984. That Seth has struck a deep chord within the collective human psyche is also evidenced in the numerous Seth-oriented seminars, study groups, and magazines, and the Sethian organizations that have sprouted up both here and around the world. As a result it should perhaps come as no surprise that Seth's many thousands of pages of dictation are now part of the permanent collection of the Yale University Archives.

In addition to the richness and seeming authenticity of Seth's unarguably fascinating pronouncements, what was doubly intriguing to me was that the lengthy dictations of a trance entity could be so coherent, original, and intelligible. After unsuccessful attempts to wring any sense out of such trance-dictated classics as William Butler Yeats's *Vision* and the famous *Urantia* book, it was both a pleasant and disconcerting surprise.

What is even more surprising is that trance entities are suddenly starting to pop up everywhere. Not only do many of them seem to be as levelheaded and eerily wise as Seth, but they are also attracting increasing numbers of followers. For example, in the early 1970s an otherwise normal businessman named Jack Pursel started channeling an entity named Lazaris. Like Seth, Lazaris also has much to say about the reincarnation process—although unlike Seth, Lazaris claims never to have experienced physical existence upon the Earth. Like Seth, Lazaris also has accumulated quite a following for himself, and a few minutes spent listening to the maturity and eerie wisdom that comes through on any one of the many Lazaris tapes quickly reveals why.

Psychologist Kathryn Ridall says that she became convinced that there was something important going on in the trance medium phenomenon after sending a year listening to the teachings of an entity named Diya who speaks through a Bay Area sensitive named Richard Ryal.[10] And since 1981 a midwesterner named Mark Zweigler has had an entity speaking through him who calls itself Jacob. Indeed, there is currently such a deluge of provocative and interesting trance material being delivered through various channelers around the country that Roberts's longtime editor Tam Mossman has founded a magazine devoted to exploring the phenomenon, *Metapsychology: The Journal of Discarnate Intelligence.*

According to Mossman the trance medium phenomenon is on the rise: "This does seem to be something that's widespread and, yes, it's increasing by leaps and bounds. Also the material's getting better. A lot of the early trance stuff I saw was pretty god-awful—a lot of the stuff you see still is—and yet a lot of the material now is good enough that I can put together a whole journal from amateurs."[11]

Mossman knows whereof he speaks. After seven years of watching Roberts go into trance, he started going into trances himself and has since become the channel for an entity named James. As he explains, James first appeared one evening in 1975 while Mossman was sitting around after dinner with friends in New York: "All of a sudden I felt like a rheostat was being turned down. My consciousness was just being pushed down. I had put myself into trances before, but this was different. Something *else* was turning me down. So I got where I needed to go. I got very small—that's the best way I can put it—and everything just tightened up into a little point of consciousness. Then I started to speak, and slowly my voice changed."[12]

The first thing the entity did after manifesting in Mossman was to turn to one of Mossman's friends and say, "You can speak for me too if you want." Days later, the man who had been addressed also went into trance, and found the entity starting to speak through him. After a few moments, it then resumed speaking through Mossman, and when it did this, Mossman's astonished friends asked what the entity would like to be called. On being informed by the entity that it didn't matter what they called it, one of Mossman's friends chose the name "James" at random, and James the entity has been ever since.

In subsequent trance sessions James has revealed that like many such alleged discarnate entities he is a plurality of beings, a gestalt of consciousness that now inhabits a nonphysical level of reality that is no longer subject to the bounds of time. Although it is difficult for those of us who are still constrained by time to imagine what timelessness would be like, James alleges that because he is through with incarnating in a linear time frame, he can actually be viewed as Tam Mossman's future self. Or in James's own words, "I am downstream of Tam, you might say—the sum total of a number of entities of whom Tam is one. Tam's experiences flow not *down* but *into* me, along with input from a wide variety of other entities and forms of consciousness. . . . In another sense . . . I am 'later' Tam. Tam is an embryonic me. And in a way quite easy for you to understand, I like to take good care of my early versions, for their 'continued' health greatly increases my own well-being and range of abilities."[13]

What Discarnate Entities Tell Us About Reincarnation

It should be stated that discarnate entities do not always agree with one another in their assessments of the reincarnation process. Similarly, many such entities also caution that their communications are more or less restricted by the vocabulary and understanding of their human channels. Nonetheless, in spite of their varying names, sources of origin, and distinct philosophical leanings, many trance entities are in surprising accordance in their overall descriptions of the mechanics of reincarnation and the after-death state.

For example, just as modern physics is beginning to assert that consciousness is intrinsic to the very reality of subatomic particles and hence the entire material universe, many discarnate entities also stress that physical reality is ultimately created by consciousness. Because it is created by consciousness, they assert that we, each of us, ultimately create our own reality and destiny through our belief systems (although they concede that the belief systems which sculpt our destinies include not only our conscious precepts and understandings, but also our unconscious ones, including those that we still allow to influence us from past lives).

Our creation of our own reality is ultimately the basis of karma as well. In this view past-life phobias, fears, worries, and guilt continue to sculpt and shape our current life because they are embedded in our unconscious belief systems about ourselves. For instance, if you have a past-life memory of having robbed someone and do not make peace with this memory in some positive and productive way, you may continue to believe that you are unworthy and deserve to be punished. This belief would be responsible for any apparent karmic punishment you experienced. In other words, there is no such thing as cosmic punishment. There is only self-punishment, which can always be ameliorated by accessing and changing outworn belief systems. Similarly, our current and future reality is also programmed and created by our beliefs and attitudes.

Discarnate entities have thought-provoking things to say about many of the other aspects of reincarnation as well. For instance, Seth asserts that our present concept of the soul "is a 'primitive' idea that can scarcely begin to explain the creativity or reality from which mankind's being comes."[14] The basic picture that Seth, James, and many other discarnate entities offer instead is that, although each human entity does possess a certain integrity and wholeness, which is roughly analogous to possessing an individual soul, ultimately we are beings without borders, complex and constantly fluctuating systems of impulses, self-awareness, and propensities, which are in turn part of a dauntingly vast spiritual ecology, a complex and infinitely interpenetrating ocean of consciousness, that permeates not only all corners of our own universe, but numerous other universes and timeless realms as well.

Because of the complexity of this intricately interlocking spiritual ecosystem, and because it encompasses realities in which space and time as we know them cease to exist, the answers that discarnate entities give to questions about the mechanics of reincarnation are often startling. For example, many discarnate entities assert that far from being frozen in a linear sequence of time, our past lives are actually occurring *simultaneously*, and it is only our belief that the past is frozen and unalterable that keeps us from realizing that at an unconscious level we are communicating with our past and future selves all of the time.

To emphasize this point, rather than use the term *past lives* James suggests that we employ the term *adjacent lives*, for, as he explains, the life that is affecting us the most at any given moment may not be our most recent incarnation, but can be any one of our multitude of existences, no matter how seemingly remote in what we currently perceive as space and time. Indeed, he asserts that instead of being laid out in a neat line, our various incarnations are actually part of a much more active and unstable arrangement. As he explains, "The easiest analogy to imagine is a roll of pennies, each with a different consecutive date from 1800 to 1985, all stacked in chronological order. Some exuberant, youthful hand knocks over the stack, and the coins roll and scatter, coming to rest everywhere—atop each other, next to one another, heads up or down. 1896 may be right next to 1930. 1815 may lie atop

1964. 1918 may have rolled off under the bureau, and never be heard from again. And so it is with your lives, your incarnations. The greater being that is your Oversoul is constantly rattling the spare change in its pockets, and so your 'present' life is constantly coming into contact with other past *and* future lives that may be quite distant in terms of chronological time, but extraordinarily intimate in terms of their psychological presence."[15]

According to James it is when two of these coins, or past lives, stick together that problems surface such as those that come to the fore during a past-life regression. By realizing that we can "berth" next to any past or adjacent life that we choose, we can access positive past-life influences and experiences.

In a recent conversation, James gently chided me for limiting my focus only to the subject of past or adjacent lives and specifically requested that I include another point in this book. He feels that it is important for human beings to know that we are affected by more than just our own past incarnations. Just as we are constantly and unconsciously extending our "psychic roots" into our various adjacent lives, because we are so interconnected with the living fabric of the universe, we are also extending our roots into even stranger places, into the gestalt consciousness or *zeitgeist* of the various historical eras we have inhabited in previous incarnations, into the impressions and feelings of people who are near to us emotionally or psychically, and even into various "nonhuman sources of nourishment." As James puts it, given the right conditions and psychic urgencies "you can be more in touch with a trilobite than you can be with your most 'recent Victorian existence' if you learn more from your sojourn into the trilobite world. You notice I did not say 'your life as a trilobite.' You notice I said 'your sojourn in the trilobite world.' "[16]

Thus, according to James, we possess the ability to do far more than just access and learn from our own adjacent lives. If we truly desire to open the floodgates of our experience, we can do so through the "total approval and appreciation" of our fellow beings. As he puts it, "That is the secret. That is why they say that love is the key. Indeed, it is. For once you love what your fellow human beings are and can do whatever they do, then you open it up to where you are able to feel, drink from, be nourished by their experiences as well as your own in lives that you have not yet begun to live."[17]

Discarnate entities such as Seth and James have much more to say about the workings of reincarnation, the afterdeath state, the nature of the psyche, but the model of spiritual reality they offer is far too rich and extensive to present here in its entirety. However, if any of the foregoing information has piqued your interest, and you would like to explore the subject of discarnate entities further, I highly recommend any of the Seth books and the Lazaris tapes. A sample copy of *Metapsychology: The Journal of Discarnate Intelligence* can be obtained for six dollars by writing: Metapsychology, The Journal of Discarnate Intelligence, P.O. Box 3295, Charlottesville, Virginia 22903.

In addition to articles on and by many of the better trance information sources extant today, one especially noteworthy feature of the journal is a question and answer section in which questions pertaining to past lives, and other subjects such as politics, personal development, and paranormal phenomena are asked of different discarnate entities and their answers are compared. The questions are not personal but are of general interest, and the answers compiled from public channeling demonstrations and seminars as well as private sessions. The addresses for contributing trance channelers who do private consultations and past-life readings are also listed in the journal.

Although it is obvious that further research is required to determine authenticity of trance information sources, at the very least the pronouncements of discarnate entities provide interesting working hypotheses for some of the greatest mystical questions of all time. Similarly, if research shows that discarnate entities are nothing more than manifestations of the unconscious minds of their channelers, the data we gather on this phenomenon cannot help but teach us more about ourselves and the mysterious workings of the human brain.

However, if discarnate entities turn out to be what they

claim, such a discovery would have implications far greater than Columbus's discovery of the New World, or even humankind's first step on the moon. In short, we may be forced to completely reassess our image of ourselves and our role in the cosmos. Put another way, we may be forced to heed the words of an unnamed discarnate entity channeled by a Philadelphia-based actor named Doug Wing: "You are part of a vaster reality, part of a vaster and greater you, more than the sum of all your parts—and less than you can be. You are more involved in your own existence than your conscious reality has allowed you to believe. You are a vaster personality than will fit within the belief systems of your known world—more than could possibly be envisioned by the science of your day and your present reality. . . . Therefore, you must strive to enlarge your mold, your cast of belief, and begin to understand the greater potential and meaning of your present existence. Make an effort to believe in your own greater reality, and you will begin on a journey of wonder [that] will reveal more than you can presently believe."[18]

Endnotes

1. Conversation with Mary Palermo, January 16, 1986.

2. Conversation with Carol Dryer, January 15, 1986.

3. Paramahansa Yogananda, *Autobiography of a Yogi* (Los Angeles: Self-Realization Fellowship, 1946), p. 188.

4. Ibid.

5. Dick Sutphen, *You Were Born Again to Be Together* (New York: Pocket Books, 1976), p. 16.

6. Dr. Adrian Finkelstein, *Your Past Lives and the Healing Process* (Farmingdale, New York: Coleman Publishing, 1985), p. 54.

7. Lawrence LeShan, *Alternate Realities* (New York: M. Evans, 1976), p. 177.

8. Lawrence LeShan, "Toward a General Theory of Psychic

Healing," in *Psychiatry and Mysticism*, ed. Stanley R. Dean, M.D. (Chicago: Nelson-Hall, 1975), p. 249.

9. Kathryn Ridall, Ph.D., "Close Encounters of a Fourth Kind: Working with Non-Incarnated Entities," *Metapsychology: The Journal of Discarnate Intelligence* 1, no. 2 (Summer 1985): 27–30.

10. Ibid.

11. Conversation with Tam Mossman, March 2, 1986.

12. Ibid.

13. "Questions and Answers," *Metapsychology: The Journal of Discarnate Intelligence* 1, no.1 (Spring 1985): 3.

14. Jane Roberts, notes and introduction by Robert F. Butts, *The "Unknown" Reality: A Seth Book*, Volume 1 (Englewood Cliffs, New Jersey: Prentice-Hall, 1977), p.78.

15. "Questions and Answers," *Metapsychology: The Journal of Discarnate Intelligence* 1, no. 2 (Summer 1985): 52.

16. Conversation with James speaking through Tam Mossman, March 2, 1986.

17. Ibid.

18. "Questions and Answers," *Metapsychology: The Journal of Discarnate Intelligence* 1, no. 2 (Summer 1985): 56.

Part Four:

Closing Words

10 ~ The Dangers of Past-Life Exploration

On several occasions throughout this book I have stressed that traumatic past-life memories should only be explored under the guidance of a trained past-life therapist. To enable you to avoid such memories in your explorations, I have provided various safeguards, such as the guardian figure and white light exercises. However, memories of extremely traumatic events are not the only dangers that you may encounter as you unravel the secrets of your own reincarnational past. For example, you may uncover a past life in which you were a thief or a miser, or a previous incarnation in which you were ill-treated or even murdered by someone you now know. If these are not dealt with in a healthy manner, such discoveries can lead to feelings of guilt, fear, and resentment toward family members and friends.

There are several ways of turning these discoveries into positive experiences. If you do not believe in the reality of past lives, view the memory that you have uncovered as an allegory or a symbolic message, much the same as the situations encountered in a dream. For example, if you dream that you catch your spouse in the act of stealing something from you, it does not necessarily mean you think your spouse is literally a thief. It may be your unconscious mind's way of telling you that you harbor some repressed hostility toward your spouse, or that you feel your spouse is relying on you too heavily in some matter. Invariably, the best way to deal with the dream is to search your own feelings for the source of the image, and then discuss the matter openly with the person in question instead of suppressing it so that it manifests only in the symbolic landscape of your dreams. This approach can also be employed with troubling past-life memories.

For instance, if you dream you recall a past life as a miser, ask yourself what the image of a miser represents to you. Then examine yourself and try to determine what you are being miserly about? It may be money or material possessions, or it may be time, affection, or compliments. Above all, don't just feel guilty over finding out that you view yourself as a miser. Your unconscious mind gave you the information because at some level you decided that it was a part of yourself that you wanted to change. Use the information to institute that change.

If you believe in the reality of reincarnation, then it is even more crucial that you do not allow unpleasant discoveries to result in feelings of guilt, fear, or resentment. If we have all lived many dozens or even hundreds of incarnations, it is only logical to expect that each of us has been, at one time or another, a murderer, a thief, a miser, a prostitute, and a traitor—just as we have also lived many lives of kindness and generosity and honesty. According to many belief systems that accept the reality of reincarnation, the purpose of this panoramic existence is not to fill the individual with guilt and remorse but to allow the soul to grow, to teach it to view life from every angle.

As was suggested in the previous chapter, negative emotions appear to be the only cause of whatever "punishment" we experience as a result of our wrongful actions. Again, the overriding lesson is that we are not meant to suffer because of our misdeeds, but to learn from them and integrate what we have learned into our current life.

A good example of how to deal with an unpleasant memory is given by California parapsychologist and past-life therapist Dr. Jeffrey Mishlove. During a state of past-life awareness, Mishlove remembered a life as a Japanese warlord, a "petty tyrant." Had he dealt with the memory in an unhealthy manner, he might have allowed himself to be racked by guilt, but instead he chose to integrate the memory. As he states, "In the therapeutic process I was able to see that even this seemingly despicable lifetime was part of a larger purpose and that much good came of it. Therefore I came to accept myself as having done these things without feeling any guilt and also fully prepared to accept my vestiges of karmic consequences which may remain to be satisfied."[1]

This is how any unpleasant memory should be dealt with. Instead of allowing it to cause further pain, defuse it. If you find that someone has done you wrong in a past life, forgive them. If you find that you did something wrong, forgive yourself and integrate what you have learned into your current experience. See all seeming evils in a larger context of learning and growth.

Although not as extreme as other problems, another danger of past-life exploration is simple intellectual disorientation. Many researchers report that even after they accept the basic premise of reincarnation, the anomalies and surprises they continue to discover while investigating the past-life phenomenon seem never ending. These include journeys to parallel universes, accounts of spirit possession, and many other bizarre occurrences.

Even putting aside such anomalies, the basic "renincarnation cosmology" people report while in a state of past-life awareness seldom matches their conscious beliefs about reincarnation. There are several ways of resolving this problem. One can deny the validity of all information reported while in states of past-life awareness. One can accept part of it and reject other parts, and try not to lose too much sleep over the arbitrariness of one's decision. Or one can accept the simple truth—that there is no single correct picture of reality, only a multitude of different pictures. This is the point of view argued by University of Massachusetts astronomer Edward Harrison in his book *The Masks of the Universe*. He maintains that we can never arrive at a single and correct picture of the universe, only a series of changing models of it.

In their book *Einstein's Space & Van Gogh's Sky*, Lawrence LeShan and physicist Henry Margenau offer a similar point of view and even address directly the complicated issue of altered states of consciousness. As they see it, one of the gravest challenges facing the human race is to learn to accept that different "domains" of experience—such as waking experience or a state of past-life awareness—have always and will always provide us with radically different pictures of reality. LeShan and Margenau argue eloquently that we should not try to determine which one is correct, but accept both for what they are, different facets of this incredibly multifaceted universe in which we live.

LeShan and Margenau believe that it is crucial for our growth as human beings to learn how to shift from waking experience into altered states of consciousness without being bothered by the disparity between the different views of reality offered by each. They state, "All the evidence we have is that this shifting is essential to us. Certainly it is universal, it occurs in every culture and in every age we know of. If we encourage the use of alternate realities, as in meditation, play, serious music, and so forth, we increase the ability of human beings to reach toward new potentials. If we prevent it, we damage these people."[2]

Thus, if you find that the picture of reality you discover in states of past-life awareness is different from the one you have grown accustomed to in your waking state, do not be too disturbed that you cannot hammer the two together. Parts of them may overlap, and other parts may not. Accept only the useful parts of each and don't worry about the rest. Or, in the words of Zen Buddhism, accept without accepting, and believe without believing.

Endnotes

1. Conversation with Jeffrey Mishlove, February 27, 1987.

2. Lawrence LeShan and Henry Margenau, *Einstein's Space & Van Gogh's Sky* (New York: Macmillan, 1982), p. 12.

Bibliography

Anderson-Evangelista, Anita. *Hypnosis.* New York: Arco Publishing, 1980.

Arroyo, Stephen. *Astrology, Karma, and Transformation.* Reno, Nevada: CRCS Publications, 1978.

Banerjee, H.N. *Americans Who Have Been Reincarnated.* New York: Macmillan, 1980.

——. *The Once and Future Life.* New York: Dell, 1979.

Benson, Herbert. *The Relaxation Response.* New York: William Morrow & Co., 1975.

Berg, Dr. Philip S. *The Wheels of the Soul.* New York: The Research Centre of Kabbalah, 1984.

Bhaktivedanta, A.C., and Prabhupada, Swami. *Coming Back.* Los Angeles: The Bhaktivedanta Book Trust, 1982.

Brennan, J.H. *Reincarnation: Five Keys to Past Lives.* Wellingborough, Northamptonshire: The Aquarian Press, 1981.

Castaneda, Carlos. *Tales of Power.* New York: Simon & Schuster, 1974.

Cayce, Hugh Lynn. *Edgar Cayce's Story of Karma.* New York: Berkley Books, 1971.

Cerminara, Gina. *Many Lives, Many Loves.* Marina del Rey, California: DeVorss & Company, 1963.

——. *Many Mansions.* New York: New American Library, 1967.

Chang, Garma C.C. *Teachings of Tibetan Yoga.* Secaucus, New Jersey: The Citadel Press, 1974.

Clow, Barbara Hand. *Eye of the Centaur.* St. Paul, Minnesota: Llewellyn Publications, 1986.

Cranston, Sylvia, and Williams, Carey. *Reincarnation: A New Horizon in Science, Religion, and Society.* New York: Julian Press, 1984.

Crowley, Aleister. *Magick.* New York: Weiser, 1979.

Dean, Stanley R., ed. *Psychiatry & Mysticism.* Chicago: Nelson-Hall, 1975.

Dethlefsen, Thornwald. *Voices from Other Lives.* New York: Evans, 1977.

Ebon, Martin, ed. *Reincarnation in the Twentieth Century.* New York: New American Library, 1969.

Erickson, Milton H., and Rossi, Ernest L., and Rossi, Sheila I. *Hypnotic Realities.* New York: Irvington Publishers, 1976.

Evans-Wentz, W.Y. *The Tibetan Book of the Great Liberation.* London: Oxford University Press, 1968.

Faraday, Ann. *Dream Power.* New York: Berkley Books, 1972.

Finkelstein, Adrian. *Your Past Lives and the Healing Process.* Farmingdale, New York: Coleman Publishing, 1985.

Fiore Dr, Edith. *You Have Been Here Before.* New York: Ballantine Books, 1978.

Fisher, Joe. *The Case for Reincarnation.* New York: Bantam Books, 1985.

Fremantle, Francesca, and Trungpa, Chogyam. *The Tibetan Book of the Dead.* Boulder, Colorado: Shambhala, 1975.

Gallup, George. *Adventures in Immortality.* New York: McGraw-Hill Book Company, 1982.

Garfield, Patricia. *Creative Dreaming.* New York: Ballantine Books, 1974.

Ghose, Sri Chinmoy Kumar. *Yoga and the Spiritual Life.* New York: Tower Publications, 1970.

Glaskin, G. M. *Windows of the Mind.* New York: Delacorte Press, 1974.

Goldberg, Dr. Bruce. *Past Lives, Future Lives.* North Hollywood, California: Newcastle Publishing, 1982.

Grant, Joan. *Far Memory.* New York: Harper and Row, 1956.

Grof, Stanislav. *Beyond the Brain.* Albany, New York: The State University of New York Press, 1985.

——. *Realms of the Human Unconscious.* New York: E.P. Dutton, 1976.

Guirdham, Arthur. *The Cathars and Reincarnation.* London: Neville Spearman, 1970.

——. *We Are One Another.* Wellingborough, Northamptonshire: Turnstone Press Limited, 1982.

Head, Joseph, and Cranston, S.L. *Reincarnation in World Thought*. New York: Julian Press, 1967.

Hilgard, Ernest R. *The Experience of Hypnosis*. New York: Harcourt, Brace & World, 1968.

Hoffman, Enid. *Develop Your Psychic Skills*. Gloucester, Massachusetts: Para Research, 1981.

Holzer, Hans. *Life Beyond Life*. West Nyack, New York: Parker Publishing Company, 1985.

Humphreys, Christmas. *Buddhism*. England: Penguin Books, 1967.

——. *Karma and Rebirth*. London: John Murray, 1943.

Iverson, Jeffery. *More Lives than One?* New York: Warner Books, 1976.

Johnston, Charles. *The Memory of Past Births*. New York: Metaphysical Publishing, 1899.

Johnson, Don. *The Protean Body*. New York: Harper & Row, 1977.

Jyotirmayananda, Swami (translated and edited by Lilian K. Donat). *Meditate the Tantric Yoga Way*. New York: E. P. Dutton & Co., 1973.

Kelly, Sean F., and Kelly, Reid J. *Hypnosis: Understanding How It Can Work For You*. Reading, Massachusetts: Addison-Wesley, 1985.

Kelsey, Denys, and Grant, Joan. *Many Lifetimes*. Garden City, New York: Doubleday, 1967.

Kohler, Wolfgang. *Gestalt Psychology*. New York: New American Library, 1947.

LaBerge, Stephen. *Lucid Dreaming*. Los Angeles: Jeremy P. Tarcher, Inc., 1985.

LeCron, Leslie M. *Self Hypnotism*. New York: New American Library, 1964.

Lenz, Frederick. *Lifetimes*. New York: Fawcett Books, 1979.

LeShan, Lawrence. *Alternate Realities*. New York: Evans, 1976.

LeShan Lawrence, and Margenau, Henry. *Einstein's Space and Van Gogh's Sky*. New York: Macmillan, 1982.

Lethbridge, T.C. *The Power of the Pendulum*. London: Routledge & Kegan Paul, 1976.

Lilly, John. *The Center of the Cyclone*. New York: Bantam Books, 1973.

Montgomery, Ruth. *Here and Hereafter*. New York: Coward-McCann, Inc., 1968

——. *Threshold To Tomorrow*. New York: Fawcett Crest, 1982.

Moore, Marcia. *Hypersentience*. New York: Bantam Books, 1977.

Moore, Marcia, and Alltounian, Howard. *Journeys Into the Bright World*. Rockport, Massachusetts: Para Research, 1978.

Moss, Peter, and Keeton, Joe. *Encounters with the Past*. Garden City, New York: Doubleday, 1981.

Naranjo, Claudio, and Ornstein, Robert E. *On the Psychology of Meditation*. New York: Viking, 1971.

Netherton, Morris, and Shiffrin, Nancy. *Past Lives Therapy*. New York: Ace Books, 1978.

Ornstein, Robert E., ed. *The Nature of Human Consciousness*. New York: Viking, 1973.

Pearce, Joseph Chilton. *Magical Child Matures*. New York: E. P. Dutton & Co., 1985.

Pearson, Durk, and Shaw, Sandy. *Life Extension*. New York: Warner Books, 1982.

Perls, Frederick, and Hefferline, Ralph E., and Goodman, Paul. *Gestalt Therapy*. New York: Bantam Books, 1977.

Polster, Erving, and Polster, Miriam. *Gestalt Therapy Integrated*. New York: Vintage, 1973.

Prabhavananda, Swami, and Isherwood, Christopher. *How to Know God: The Yoga Aphorisms of Patanjali*. New York: New American Library, 1953.

Progoff, Ira. *The Practice of Process Meditation*. New York: Dialogue House Library, 1980.

Rajneesh, Bhagwan Shree. *Meditation*. New York: Harper & Row, 1978.

Ring, Kenneth. *Heading Toward Omega*. New York: William Morrow, 1985.

Rogo, D. Scott. *The Search for Yesterday*. Englewood Cliffs, New Jersey: Prentice-Hall, 1985.

Roberts, Jane. *How to Develop Your ESP Power*. New York: Pocket Books, 1966.

———. *Seth Speaks*. New York: Bantam Books, 1972.

———. *The Nature of Personal Reality*. New York: Bantam Books, 1978.

———. *The Nature of the Psyche*. New York: Bantam Books, 1984.

———. *The Seth Material*. Englewood Cliffs, New Jersey: Prentice-Hall, 1970.

———. *The "Unknown" Reality: A Seth Book.* (2 volumes), Englewood Cliffs, New Jersey: Prentice-Hall, 1979.

Stearn, Jess. *Soul Mates.* New York: Bantam Books, 1984.

———. *Yoga, Youth, and Reincarnation.* New York: Bantam Books, 1965.

Steiger, Brad, and Steiger, Frances. *The Love Force.* Englewood Cliffs, New Jersey: Prentice-Hall, 1985.

Stein, Murray, ed. *Jungian Analysis.* Boulder, Colorado: Shambhala, 1984.

Steiner, Rudolf. *Reincarnation and Karma.* London: Rudolf Steiner Press, 1977.

Stevens, Petey. *Opening Up to Your Psychic Self.* Berkeley, California: Nevertheless Press, 1983.

Stevenson, Ian. *Telepathic Impressions.* Charlottesville, Virginia: The University Press of Virginia, 1970.

———. *Twenty Cases Suggestive of Reincarnation.* Charlottesville, Virginia: The University Press of Virginia, 1974.

———. *Xenoglossy.* Charlottesville, Virginia: The University Press of Virginia, 1974.

Storr, Anthony, ed. *The Essential Jung.* Princeton, New Jersey: Princeton University Press, 1983.

Sutphen, Dick, and Taylor, Lauren Leigh. *Past-Life Therapy in Action.* Malibu, California: Valley of the Sun Publishing Co., 1983.

———. *Past Lives, Future Loves.* New York: Pocket Books, 1978.

———. *Unseen Influences.* New York: Pocket Books, 1982.

———. *You Were Born Again to be Together.* New York: Pocket Books, 1976.

Talbot, Michael. *Beyond the Quantum.* New York: Macmillan, 1986.

———. *Mysticism and the New Physics.* New York: Bantam Books, 1981.

———. *The Delicate Dependency.* New York: Avon Books, 1982.

Tart, Charles, ed. *Altered States of Consciousness.* New York: John Wiley & Sons, 1969.

Thera, Nyanaponika. *The Heart of Buddhist Meditation.* New York: Samuel Weiser, 1965.

Trungpa, Chogyam. *Born in Tibet.* Boston: Shambhala, 1985.

Van Waveren, Erlo. *Pilgrimage to Rebirth.* New York: Samuel Weiser, 1978.

Wambach, Helen. *Life Before Life.* New York: Bantam Books, 1979.

——. *Reliving Past Lives.* New York: Barnes & Noble Books, 1984.

Wilson, Ian. *All in the Mind.* Garden City, New York: Doubleday, 1981.

Williston, Glenn, and Johnstone, Judith. *Soul Search.* Wellingborough, Northamptonshire: The Aquarian Press, 1983.

Wolf, Fred. *Star Wave.* New York: Macmillan, 1984.

Wolberg, Lewis R. *Hypnosis: Is it for You?* New York: Dembner Books, 1982.

Yogananda, Paramahansa. *Man's Eternal Quest.* Los Angeles: Self-Realization Fellowship, 1982.

Credits

Grateful acknowledgment is hereby made to the following for permission to quote selections from previously published material:

Einstein's Space and Van Gogh's Sky by Lawrence LeShan and Henry Margenau. Copyright © 1982 by Lawrence LeShan and Henry Margenau. All rights reserved. Used by permission of the Macmillan Publishing Company, a division of Macmillan, Inc.

The Heart of Buddhist Meditation by Nyanaponika Thera. Copyright © 1962 by Nyanaponika Thera. All rights reserved. Used by permission of Samuel Weiser, Inc.

The Joyous Cosmology: Adventures in the Chemistry of Consciousness by Alan W. Watts. Copyright © 1966 by Alan W. Watts. All rights reserved. Used by permission of Pantheon Books, a division of Random House, Inc.

"Kay Ortman's Way" by My, from *Human Behavior*, May 1979. Copyright © 1974 by *Human Behavior*. All rights reserved. Used by permission of *Human Behavior*.

Life Beyond Life by Hans Holzer. Copyright © 1985 by Hans Holzer. All rights reserved. Used by permission of Parker Publishing Company, Inc.

Life Extension by Durk Pearson and Sandy Shaw. Copyright ©

1982 by Durk Pearson and Sandy Shaw. All rights reserved. Used by permission of Warner Books, Inc.

Man's Eternal Quest by Paramahansa Yogananda. Copyright © 1975, 1982 by Self-Realization Fellowship. All rights reserved. Used by permission of Self-Realization Fellowship.

Many Lives, Many Loves by Gina Cerminara. Copyright © 1963 by Gina Cerminara. All rights reserved. Used by permission of DeVorss & Company.

Memories, Dreams, and Reflections by C. G. Jung. Copyright © 1961, 1962, 1963 by Random House, Inc. Translated by Richard and Clara Winston, recorded and edited by Aniela Jaffe. Used by permission of Pantheon Books, a division of Random House, Inc.

"Questions and Answers," from *Metapsychology*, Spring 1985. Copyright © 1985 by *Metapsychology*. All rights reserved. Used by permission of *Metapsychology*.

Pilgrimage to the Rebirth by Erlo van Waveren. Copyright © 1978 by Erlo van Waveren. All rights reserved. Used by permission of Samuel Weiser, Inc.

"President's Message," by Ernest F. Pecci, M.D., from *The Association for Past-Life Research and Therapy Newsletter*, Spring 1984. Copyright © 1984 by The Association for Past-Life Research and Therapy. All rights reserved. Used by permission of Ernest F. Pecci, M.D.

The Search for Yesterday by D. Scott Rogo. Copyright © 1985 by D. Scott Rogo. All rights reserved. Used by permission of Prentice-Hall, Inc.

You Have Been Here Before by Edith Fiore. Copyright © 1978 by Edith Fiore. All rights reserved. Used by permission of Coward, McCann & Geoghegan, a division of the Putnam Publishing Group.

Index

active imagination, 67–69, 117–121
adjacent lives, 151–153
alarm clocks, 60–61
altered states of consciousness, 81, 97, 98, 162
Alternate Realities (LeShan), 146
American Psychiatric Association, 146
animals, 10, 42
archaeology, 47–48
art, 35–36
aspartame, 61
Association for Past-Life Research and Therapy, 126–127
Association for the Psychophysiological Study of Sleep, 69
Association of Psychic Practitioners, 137
astrology, 143–145
  karma and, 144
atmosphere, 21–22, 85
Autobiography of a Yogi (Yogananda), 143–144

Beyond the Quantum (Talbot), 4
Bible, 91
Blofeld, John, 69
body karmas, 43
Born in Tibet (Trungpa), 37
brain, 97–98
Buddhism, 2, 37,78

candles, 24, 86, 99–100
Castaneda, Carlos, 71–72
Cayce, Edgar, 143
Cerminara, Gina, 77
Chang, Garma C. C., 71, 72–73
channeling, *see* trance entities
children, past-life memories of, 1–2, 34–35, 36–37, 41, 43–44
Christos Technique, 24, 112–116
chronological record, 16
climate, 42
"Close Encounters of a Fourth Kind" (Ridall), 146
clothing, 38–39
Clow, Barbara, 8–9
Cohen, Pamela, 55–56
consciousness, reality as, 150
Creative Dreaming (Garfield), 63
cruelty, in past lives, 19

Dalai Lama, 36–37
David-Neel, Alexandra, 37
déjà vu, 29, 30
Delicate Dependency, The (Talbot), 3

Denning, Hazel, 9, 126, 127
discussion groups, 62
Diya, 148
don Juan, 72
"Dr. Who," 92
dream images, 117–118
Dreams: Discovering Your Inner Teacher (Reid), 57
dreams, past-life, 21, 24–26, 52–76, 132, 160
  continuation of, 67–69
  discussion of, 62–63
  guardian figures in, 73–74
  hypnotic, 96–97
  lucid, 69–74
  meaning of, 56–57
  painful, 64
  programming for, 63–66
  recognition of, 55–56
  recurring, 56
  symbolism in, 65, 68
  techniques for remembering, 57–63
drugs, 25, 58
Dryer, Carol, 8, 112, 138, 141

eating disorders, 6
Einstein, Albert, 10
Einstein's Space & Van Gogh's Sky (LeShan & Margenau), 162
electroencephalograms (EEGs), 96–97
elevator meditation, 92
Essential Balm, 24
Eye of the Centaur (Clow), 9
eyes, 44

family, 46, 62–63
fear, 78–79
Fenelon, 54–55
finger movements, 49–50
Finkelstein, Adrian, 144
Fiore, Edith, 6
food, 41
  dream-encouraging, 61–62
fraud, 140–141, 146
Freud, Sigmund, 81
friends, 62–63, 108
  in past lives, 46, 66
furniture, 38, 39

Garfield, Patricia, 63, 74
gender, 5, 45
geography, in past lives, 4–5, 28–30, 32–33
gestalt, 149, 152
Gestalt psychology, 132–133
Glaskin, Gerry, 112
Goldwater, Richard, 60
Grof, Stanislav, 7
group hypnotism, 4, 131–132
guardian figures, 73–74, 81–83, 89–90, 108, 109
  explanations of, 82–83
guided meditation, 107–116, 132
  basic technique for, 107–112
  Christos technique for, 112–116
guilt, 19, 160–161

habit, 16, 103
hallway meditation, 91, 110
Harrison, Edward, 162
hobbies, 34–36
Holzer, Hans, 53
Human Behavior, 134
hypnosis, 96–104
  basic technique for, 98–101
  group, 4, 131–132
  index card technique of, 103–104
  meditation compared with, 96–98
  through repeated suggestion, 101–102
  room for, 99
hypnotherapy, 128–131
  group, 131–132
  moral transgressions under, 129
  painful memories and, 131
  vividness in, 130, 131

imagination, active, 67–69, 117–121
incense, 23, 85
index cards, 24, 103–104
induction images, 88, 91–94
injuries, 7, 43, 64
istiqara, 64
Itivuttaka, 78

James, 148–149, 152–153
journals:
  dream, 57–58
  past-life, 15–21
Jue, Ronald Wong, 125
Jung, C. G., 52, 54, 67, 68

karma, 52, 144, 150
  body, 43

LeBerge, Stephen, 70–71
languages, 40
Lazaris, 148, 153
LeCron, Leslie M., 47
left brain, 97
Lenz, Frederick, 55
LeShan, Lawrence, 145–146, 162
Lethbridge, T. C., 47–48
Life Before Life (Wambach), 4
Life Extension (Pearson & Shaw), 61–62
Lifetimes (Lenz), 55–56
lighting, 22–23
Lucid Dreaming (LaBerge), 70
lucid dreams, 69–74

Magic and Mystery in Tibet (David-Neel), 37
Man's Eternal Quest (Yogananda), 27
Many Lives, Many Loves (Cerminara), 77
Margenau, Henry, 162
Marlowe, Frank, 130
Masks of the Universe, The (Harrison), 162
massage, 113, 134
meditation, 20–21, 54, 77–95
  basics of, 84–87
  for dreaming, 58–60
  guided, 107–116, 132
  hypnotism compared with, 96–98
  past-life, 88–91
  room for, 21–24
  safeguards for, 78–84
Memories, Dreams, Reflections (Jung), 52
mentholated salve, 24, 113
Metaphysical and Parapsychological Institute, 138
Metapsychology: The Journal of Discarnate Intelligence, 148, 153
mirror meditation, 93–94
mirrors, 24
Mishlove, Jeffrey, 161
Mnemonic Induction of Lucid Dreams (MILD), 70–71
Mossman, Tam, 148–149
music, 23, 35
Mysticism and the New Physics (Talbot), 4, 147

native Americans, 74
near-death experiences (NDEs), 81
Netherton, Morris, 132–134
Netherton Method, 132–134
New Times, 112
Newton, Isaac, 10
New York Spiritualists Center, Inc., 138
NutraSweet, 61

occupations, 39–40
Ojibwa, 74
Ortman, Kay, 134

painful memories, 64, 78–79, 80, 102, 111, 131, 159–162
Palermo, Mary, 137–138

past-life exploration:
through active imagination, 117–121
through astrology, 143–145
clearing body for, 24–25
dangers of, 159–162
through dreaming, 52–74
through guided meditation, 107–116
through hypnosis, 96–104
through meditation, 77–95, 107–116
methods of, 20–21
preparing for, 15–26
with psychics, 136–143
Resonance Method of, 20–21, 25, 27–50
room for, 21–24
through therapy, 6, 125–135
trance entities and, 145–154
past-life memories:
of children, 1–2, 34–35, 36–37, 41, 43–44
as famous people, 2, 5
friends in, 46, 66
gender and, 5, 45
geography in, 4–5, 28–30, 32–33
injuries in, 7, 43, 64
objects in, 36–39
painful, 64, 78–79, 80, 102, 111, 131, 159–162
personalities in, 17–18
phobias from, 43, 150
talents and, 8–9, 18–19
time periods of, 33–34
trauma in, 19
Past Lives Therapy (Netherton & Shiffrin), 134
Patanjali, 77–78
Paxson, Gregory, 8
Pearson, Durk, 61–62
Pecci, Ernest, 82, 127–128
pendulums, 24, 47–50, 64
personality, 44–46
phenylalanine, 61
phobias, 43, 150
physical problems, 7–8
physical traits, 43–44
Pilgrimage to the Rebirth (van Waveren), 55
polio, 8
psychic abilities, 47
psychics, 136–143
accuracy of, 139
humanity of, 142–143
legitimacy of, 140–143
location of, 137–140
psychological problems, 6–7
psychology:
gestalt, 132–133
transpersonal, 81
punishment, 150, 160–161
Pursel, Jack, 148

quantum physics, 10, 147

race, 36
reality, theories of, 10–11, 150–151, 162
Reid, Clyde, 57
relaxation techniques, 58–59, 88–89, 90–91, 99, 108
religion, 41–42, 82, 143
Reliving Past Lives (Wambach), 4
repeated suggestion, 101–103
Resonance Method, 20–21, 25, 27–50
advantages of, 50
description of, 28–32
false past-life history and, 30–32
muddy fresco compared to, 31
unconscious mind and, 47–49
use of, 32–46
Ridall, Kathryn, 146, 148
right brain, 97–98
Roberts, Jane, 147
Rogo, D. Scott, 53
Ryal, Richard, 148

Search for Yesterday, The (Rogo), 53
self-hypnosis, *see* hypnosis
Self-Hypnotism (LeCron), 47
Senoi, 62–63, 74
Seth, 147–148, 151, 153
Shaw, Sandy, 61–62
Shiffrin, Nancy, 134
shrines, 22
skiing, 8
soul, 151
speech patterns, 132–134
Stevenson, Ian, 35, 36, 41, 42
Stewart, Kilton, 63
Storr, Anthony, 67
suggestibility, 98, 129
surgery, 130
Swygard, Diane and William, 112
symbolism, 65, 68, 83, 159–160

talents, past-life, 8–9, 18–19
Tantric Mysticism of Tibet (Blofeld), 69
tape recorders, 24, 67, 139–140
Teachings of Tibetan Yoga (Chang), 71
therapy, past-life, 6, 125–135
  approaches to, 128–135
  locating therapist for, 126–128
third eye region, 113
Tholey, Paul, 71
Thomson, Juanita, 53
Tibet, 36, 69
Tiger Balm, 24, 113
time machine meditation, 92
time periods, 33–34
trance entities, 145–154
  abundance of, 148–149
  adjacent lives and, 151–153
  reincarnation and, 150–154
transpersonal psychology, 81
traumas, 19
Trungpa, Chogyam, 37
tulku, 36–37
tunnel meditation, 88, 90–91

unconscious mind:
  communicating with, 16, 20, 25, 47–50, 79–80,
  goals and, 89
  as guardian figure, 81, 83
  as protective, 48, 64, 79, 89–90
  symbolism of, 65, 68, 83, 159–160
Urantia (Yeats), 148

vampires, 3
van Waveren, Ann, 54
van Waveren, Erlo, 54, 56
Vision (Yeats), 147
visualization, 87–94, 100, 110, 113–115, 117–118
vitamin B_{12}, 61–62

Wambach, Helen, 4–6, 10, 39
Waters, Craig R., 112
Wells, H. G., 92
white light, 83–84, 90
Windows of the Mind (Glaskin), 112
Wing, Doug, 154
Woolger, Jennifer, 93
Woolger, Roger, 93

Yale University Archives, 147
Yaqui Indians, 71–72
Yeats, William Butler, 147–148
yoga, 69, 77–78
Yogananda, Paramahansa, 27, 44, 143–144

Zanesville, Ohio, 53
zeitgeist, 152

About the Author

Michael Talbot is the author of two science books, MYSTICISM AND THE NEW PHYSICS and BEYOND THE QUANTUM, and three novels, THE DELICATE DEPENDENCY, THE BOG and NIGHT THINGS. Through a lifetime of study he is now able to recall twenty past lives. He lives in New York City.